No Scrap Left Behind

16 Quilt Projects That Celebrate
Scraps of All Sizes

AMANDA JEAN NYBERG

stash BOOKS.

Text and photography copyright © 2017
by Amanda Jean Nyberg

Photography and artwork copyright © 2017
by C&T Publishing, Inc.

Publisher: Amy Marson

Creative Director: Gailen Runge

Editor: Lynn Koolish

Technical Editors: Alison M. Schmidt
and Gailen Runge

Cover/Book Designer: Page + Pixel

Production Coordinator:
Zinnia Heinzmann

Production Editors: Jennifer Warren,
Nicole Rolandelli, and Jeanie German

Illustrator: Lon Eric Craven

Photo Assistants: Carly Jean Marin
and Mai Yong Vang

Style photography by Lucy Glover
and instructional photography
by Diane Pedersen and
Amanda Jean Nyberg, unless
otherwise noted

Published by Stash Books, an imprint of C&T Publishing, Inc.,
P.O. Box 1456, Lafayette, CA 94549

Library of Congress Cataloging-in-Publication Data

Names: Nyberg, Amanda Jean, 1975- author.

Title: No scrap left behind : 16 quilt projects that celebrate scraps of all sizes / Amanda Jean Nyberg.

Description: Lafayette, CA : C&T Publishing, Inc., [2017]

Identifiers: LCCN 2016030821 | ISBN 9781617453366 (soft cover)

Subjects: LCSH: Patchwork--Patterns. | Quilting--Patterns.

Classification: LCC TT835 .N925 2016 | DDC 746.46--dc23

LC record available at https://lccn.loc.gov/2016030821

Printed in the USA

10 9 8 7 6 5 4 3 2 1

Dedication

To the best family anyone could ask for:
Kevin, Zach, Parker, and Abby

Acknowledgments

First and foremost, thanks to God, my Father
and Creator … and his son, Jesus, my Savior.

Many thanks to my family—Kevin, Zach, Parker, and
Abby—who put up with all of the craziness (and
threads!) that came along with book writing. I'm so
thankful for each and every one of you.

Thanks to my friends Tara Rebman, Kristin Lawson,
Brianne Hanson, Mary Kolb, and Cheryl Arkison,
who encouraged me and offered advice behind the
scenes. Thanks for cheering me on while I sewed
in a bubble in my basement. I couldn't have done it
without you!

Thanks to Mrs. Gohmann, who helped out in a pinch
and offered the diversion of a walk at just the right
time. I'm grateful to have such a good neighbor.

Thanks to the many friends who have shared their
scraps with me over the years. (You know who you
are!) My quilts are all the better because of it.

Thanks to my pattern testers and proofreaders:
Tracy Westhoff, Nettie Peterson, Katherine Greaves,
Cheryl Arkison, Mary Kolb, and Kristin Lawson. I
appreciate your feedback more than I can say!

Many, many thanks to the readers of my blog, *crazy
mom quilts*. Without you this book would not be a
reality. Thanks for your encouragement and support
over the past decade.

Thanks to the wonderful staff at C&T Publishing,
who made this book a reality. It is a privilege to work
with you.

And last, but certainly not least, a huge thank-you
to Steffani K. Burton for doing such a wonderful job
quilting several of these quilts.

Contents

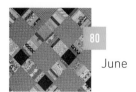

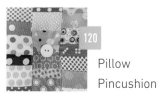

Introduction

The idea of this book has been percolating for several years. Back in 2011, right after Cheryl Arkison and I completed writing our book, *Sunday Morning Quilts* (by C&T Publishing), I was at a small quilt retreat with a few friends. Taglines were given out to each of the members during the weekend. The one that was assigned to me was "leave no scrap behind." We all laughed about it, but it sums up my quilting style perfectly. In fact, my love for using scraps seems to intensify as each year passes. I find endless enjoyment in using as many scraps as possible. I hope this book encourages and inspires you to do the same!

The quilts and projects in this book are designed to use up every last scrap. They are categorized according to different scrap shapes: squares, strings, triangles, and snippets. There are some small projects included for (nearly) instant gratification purposes, and then there are the quilts that will take a while. Making several of these quilts will be more like a marathon than a sprint, but the results are worth it in the end.

I used to have the theory that smaller scraps are great for small projects and small quilts. For this collection of quilts, however, I pushed further and dug deeper. I wanted to explore how small scraps work in bigger quilts. It takes a little more tenacity and a lot more time, but it also puts a larger dent in the scrap bin. The results are quilts that you can actually snuggle under, and that's hard to beat!

Most of us have more fabric than we know what to do with, but it doesn't seem appropriate to throw out the scraps just because of the excess. Why not make the most of all of the fabric? Scrap quilting is a great way to honor the women (and men) who have gone before us, who stitched quilts from what they had on hand and who handed down this wonderful craft to us.

I hope the projects contained in this book inspire you to actually *use* your scraps. That is my one goal! Some of you may want to make the quilts following the patterns exactly, and that's great. Some of you may want to use these quilts and projects as a jumping-off point and run with an idea of your own. That's great, too! Make the quilts your own. Make them the size and shape you want to. Be sure to put your own personal twist on them. Have fun emptying those scrap baskets.

THE
Journey

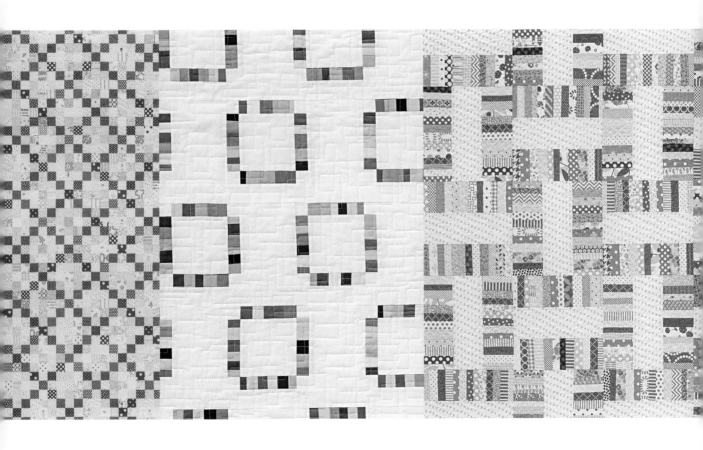

How It All Started

In the year 2000 I made my first quilt. I was pregnant with my first child, and I wanted to make him a quilt; so I bought six yards of flannel from my local Ben Franklin store. It didn't occur to me to research anything about quilting before purchasing the fabric. Thankfully I met Nancy through my church not long after my purchase. She found out that I wanted to learn how to quilt, so she invited me (and my husband) over for dinner, and afterward she gave me my first quilting lesson. It was a great arrangement all around! It took several more meetings to complete my first quilt, but Nancy helped me every step of the way. It was a very humble beginning... the quilt was just plain patchwork, but it was a start. The quilt has been used and loved, and it is still intact more than fifteen years later, so I'd call that a success! As for the rest of the original six yards of fabric, I think it made its way into at least eight quilts. I got so sick of using that fabric that I was relieved when I finally used it up!

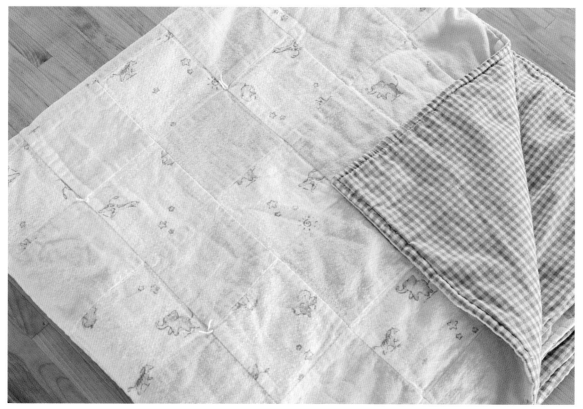

My first quilt

I was pleased with my first completed quilt, but I lacked confidence that I could take on this quilting hobby. I didn't want to invest in the supplies if it wasn't for me. So for my second quilt, I made a square cardboard template, and I cut out all my fabric pieces with a pair of not-so-sharp scissors. I made my second quilt all by myself. I was pleased that I was able to finish a quilt on my own, even if it was just a tied wallhanging. Nancy was very kind, and she encouraged my early efforts. Later that year, for my birthday, she gave me a rotary cutter, ruler, and cutting mat—I was on my way to becoming a quilter. I'm so thankful for Nancy and the time that she took to teach me how to quilt. What a difference she made in my life.

After those first two quilts, I quilted occasionally (mostly for gifts) and made a few quilts for my family. I continued to learn new skills from Nancy. She and I attended classes together, and we participated in a block-of-the-month program at our local quilt shop. I read quilting books and made lists and lists of quilts that I wanted to make. Quilting was a great creative outlet that I could accomplish in small bits while my kids napped. It was so nice to make something, and when it was done, it was done.

Early in 2006 I discovered sewing and quilting blogs. I read and absorbed all the information and inspiration I could find. A whole new world had opened up before me, and I was in awe. Fresh inspiration was available daily. I soaked up as much as I could.

Late in 2006 I started my own blog, *crazy mom quilts*. I had no idea (none!) what it would lead to, but I knew that I wanted to be a part of the community. I started by sharing the things I was working on, quilts in progress, and my completed quilts. People commented, and it was so encouraging. I "met" people from all over the world and started to develop relationships with some of them. It was fulfilling. As I posted more often, I needed to produce more content. I worked harder. I sewed faster. There was more of everything—except sleep. One year I completed 44 quilts—in a year! That pace isn't sustainable over the long haul, I can assure you.

I was not only writing on my blog but continuing to read other blogs, and I learned so much. I became a better quilter in a short time because I was picking up tips, tricks, and hints nearly every day. I was practicing my craft nearly every day, too.

The constant inspiration was great, and I was enjoying it, but it was easy to be overwhelmed by the fast pace. I began to look for my own personal style, and it was very difficult to determine what that was. I had a few patient friends who would listen to me as I bemoaned the fact that I didn't know what my style was. One friend challenged me by asking, "Does it really matter?" and "Do you need a style?" I certainly thought so.

I would watch other quilters buy new fabric. They would buy beautiful bundles of brand-new fat quarters all stacked perfectly—and they would open up that beautiful bundle and cut into it right away. Right away! I was bewildered that they could cut into new fabric while it was still new. I had a tendency to let the fabric age at least a year or two before I cut into it. Cutting into new fabric made me extremely nervous, because it was too good. I was always afraid that I would mess it up, and what a shame that would be. I also had a tendency to hoard or save it, thinking that someday a better project would come along. But cutting into new fabric seemed like the thing to do, so I tried to do the same. I made a few quilts from one fabric line while the fabric was still fairly new, and it was okay—but it felt formulaic, and I definitely felt pressure to do justice to this beautiful fabric. It wasn't fun for me, and I wasn't sure why.

Frugality and Rescuing Fabric

I grew up on a dairy farm. I was one of six kids, and my dad raised us while running a business. We didn't have a lot of extras or frivolous things, as you can probably imagine. Practicality was the name of the game. We used what we had, and we made the best of it. Those habits became deeply ingrained in me, and when I grew up I discovered that as much as I would like to change those habits at times, I couldn't easily do it.

Sometime around 2010 I realized that I would rather rescue scraps of fabric than cut into the new stuff. This realization was a huge step for me. Huge! If you gave me a tall tower of shiny new fabric, I would freeze with indecision. The possibilities are too vast, and the stakes are too high. On the other hand, if you were to hand me a bag of scraps, I would find a way to use as many of them as I could and make them into something pretty. What a fun challenge! I could work with scraps all day long, and it would energize me rather than exhaust me. When I started working with my frugal nature rather than against it, I found so much satisfaction in my work. It may sound like a simple realization, but it was a big turning point in my quilting journey.

Going Scrap Crazy

Once I discovered that I loved playing with scraps most of all, I dove in—and I dove in deep. It seemed like the crazier I became with scraps the more I enjoyed it. There were a few projects that I posted on my blog that I was a bit embarrassed about at first (because they seemed too crazy), but those were the projects that got the biggest reaction. I was finally in the sweet spot that I had been searching for. It took many years of trial and error and practice to get there, but it was worth it.

My blog readers were an integral part of the whole process. They were kind, encouraging, and enthusiastic—and they offered feedback as I worked. The work I was doing resonated with them and gave them new ideas for their scraps as well. That encouragement fueled my journey, and I'm so thankful for it.

Finding Your Niche

What I'm discovering now is that even after you find your niche, it doesn't mean that you have arrived. It's only the beginning! Creativity is a journey, and there is no destination. It's a process in which each step builds upon the last. It's a path that you will continue on, and it will change as long as you are making things. I think that's exciting.

I want to encourage you to start where you are. Practice your craft. Don't give up. Find what you love. Make the quilts that you want to make. *Make them the way you want to make them.* Have fun. Work hard. Work with your strengths, not against them. Challenge yourself to keep growing. Try new things. Never stop learning. Never stop exploring. And most importantly, **enjoy the journey!**

SCRAP
Management

Scrap quilting is a messy endeavor, and it is time consuming. But I would still pick it over all other types of quilting. There is endless potential in a pile of scraps.

Where Do All the Scraps Come From?

This is a commonly asked question, and it's a fair question. I sew a lot, so many of the scraps come from other projects that I have made. I also have a bit of a scrap reputation. Some of my quilting friends don't want to deal with their scraps—they would rather pass them along to me. This is helpful on two counts: For them, it clears up space in their sewing area. For me, I gain added variety in my scrap baskets. It's very common for quilters to gravitate to the same type, color, or style of fabric over and over when they shop, and I am no exception to that rule. I tend to buy the same kinds of things all the time. When my friends contribute to my scrap basket, the variety that is added is invaluable. When it comes to scrap quilting, variety is key.

Where Do I Start?

With regard to scraps, I hear from folks all the time, "I don't even know where to start." Sometimes there is a burden of guilt associated with that statement. Sometimes it is said out of frustration. Either way, I am here to offer hope and a solution to that pile (mountain?) of scraps.

I've often responded to the question, "Where do I start?" by saying, "Start by sorting." That isn't a bad idea at all. Yet if you have multiple boxes of scraps left over from countless projects, sorting is an intimidating venture right off the bat. If that's the case, you might want to try to select a few of your favorite scraps and make a project out of them. It doesn't need to be a big project. It can be a pillow cover, a pot holder, or even something as small as a pincushion. By getting a completed project behind you, you can enjoy the success and taste the potential results that scrap quilting can bring. Who knows—you might even find it addictive. Do this a time or two and see what happens. See how good taking action feels.

After you have created a few scrap projects, then by all means dive in and sort your scraps. It will take time, but it will feel good to have them in order.

One other recommendation that I would offer is to invite a fabric-loving friend over to help you sort. It will be a much more enjoyable task with good company, and inviting a friend will bring an element of accountability to the table as well.

Sorting and Storing

Sorting your scraps is a necessary part of the process, and how you sort them should reflect the style of your work. Early in my quilting days, I tried cutting all my scraps into squares of various sizes. Once I completed a project, the remains got chopped up into squares immediately. I stopped using that method because it seemed like I was always cutting and yet I never had the right-sized fabric in the color I needed. The process didn't work for me.

Now I like to start by sorting my scraps by color. A lot of my quilts start with choosing a color scheme, so for me sorting scraps by color is a natural choice. The majority of my scraps are stored in quilted storage boxes (the pattern can be found in *Sunday Morning Quilts* by C&T Publishing), and those boxes reside under my cutting table. There are boxes for twelve colors and one for multicolored fabrics, so thirteen boxes in all. Generally,

the scraps in these boxes are smaller than a fat quarter but larger than a charm square. If I put all my little scraps in these boxes, the boxes would need to be much larger!

For the smaller scraps, I sort by shape rather than color. The categories for these are 2½″ × 2½″ squares, snippets, triangles, and small low-volume pieces. These smaller pieces are stored in a multidrawer rolling cart.

Snippets are scraps that are smaller than 2½″ on all sides. Triangles are mostly leftover pieces from joining binding ends together, but some are trimmings from constructing quilt blocks. The small low-volume pieces belong to what I would consider a short-term category. They are various light-value fabrics that I am collecting for a special project. Once the project is finished, I won't need to separate these pieces any longer.

Quilted storage boxes

Small scrap storage

This is my **catchall basket.** The scraps in this basket may be of any color. It holds pieces that are too small to go into the color baskets but too large to put into the snippets drawer. The basket also holds strings and strips that are shorter than 6″. Basically, it's a basket of scraps that don't fit into any of the other categories. This basket is my first stop if I am making smaller projects. It's a great starting point for making things like place mats, pin-cushions, and pillow tops.

I also have a **basket just for strings** (anything that is between 1″ and 3″ wide and longer than 6″) and a separate bowl for selvages and strings that are too skinny to sew. The skinny strings (1″ wide or less) are knitted into rag rugs.

Catchall basket

Basket of strings

Selvages and strings for knitting

And lastly I have a **basket of solids**. Separating the solids from the printed fabrics is a fairly new development for me, but I find that a whole bin of solids is much more inspirational to me than solids mingled with my print scraps. This is a purely personal preference. All sizes of solid-colored scraps, except for the smallest bits, go into this basket.

I've revamped my sorting methods and honed them over the years to reflect my space and working style. My scrap categories change a bit here and there as projects are started or finished. The system is in a constant state of flux, but that's okay. In fact, that's probably why it works.

There are so many ways you can sort your scraps, but ultimately you need to have a system that is customized to you, your storage limitations, your patience, and the way in which you work.

And there are many different boxes, bins, and containers that you can use to store your scraps. If nothing else, you can rely on a trusty system of clear plastic bags that are stored in a large plastic bin. Whatever system you choose, make sure that your scraps are easily accessible. Otherwise it is unlikely that you will use them.

Basket of solids

Mixing Materials

Mustard Mishap, by Amanda Jean Nyberg

A variety of fabrics, including linen, denim, and chambray, were used in this quilt.

I recommend using 100% quilting cotton for the majority of your quilts. Using the same materials throughout sets you up for success and eliminates a lot of frustration. What about other scraps, such as denim, linen, canvas, double gauze, chambray, and so on? Can you use them in quilts, too? The answer is yes. But I recommend doing so occasionally and intentionally.

A few years ago, a friend of mine passed along a huge bag of scraps to me. The colors within each piece were subtle, but the textures were amazing. There was a variety of linen, denim, chambray, gingham, shot cotton, double gauze, and even a little bit of canvas. I used them all in one quilt. The stretch of the fabric isn't uniform throughout, but I knew that with

careful stitching, pressing, and a free-form improvisational design, I could get away with mixing all of the fabrics in one piece. I quilted it fairly densely and evenly, so if the fabrics were to shrink unevenly, the quilting would still hold the layers in place and prevent unattractive puckering. To launder, I treated it like any other quilt, washing it in cold water with a mild detergent. To dry the quilt, I used the dryer only for a short time (10–15 minutes) to eliminate the wrinkles and then laid the quilt flat to air dry. In the end, though, the quilt did shrink unevenly. It's no longer an exact rectangle, even though I squared it up after quilting. I've decided to embrace the irregular shape as part of the charm of the quilt. I like to think of it as a nod to the imperfect utility quilts that our quilting ancestors made.

MAKING
Scrap Quilts

When I start making a quilt, especially a scrap quilt, I rarely have a vision or a plan of how the whole quilt is going to look at the end. I like to start sewing and see where the project takes me. It's exciting and unpredictable—but in the best way for me. I discover new ideas when working in this manner, and it is never boring. It also means that there is a lot (*a lot*) of decision making and editing that goes on during the process.

Choosing a Color Scheme

Just because you are making a scrappy quilt doesn't mean that you have to use *all* of the colors in every quilt. It is fun to do that, definitely, but sometimes it's good to choose a few to work with and limit the color palette. For the projects in this book, I did some of each. I went all-out scrappy, as I like to call it, in *Mini Nines* (page 36), *All Sizes* (page 54), and *June* (page 80). For *Scrap Happy Rails* (page 74), I used a warm color palette of pinks, oranges, yellows, and reds. I separated the scraps into warm and cool colors for *Hot & Cold* (page 42), and I used cool colors almost exclusively in *Slopes* (page 62). *Subtle* (page 48) is a scrappy twist on a red-and-white quilt.

As you begin planning your quilt, assess the scraps that you have. What color combinations do you see right off the bat that inspire you? Which colors do you have the most of? Why not start there?

If you are stuck picking a color scheme, try these exercises:

- Think of one of your favorite places. It could be remembered from your childhood (Grandma's kitchen, a meadow in the summertime), or it could be a place you experienced on a vacation that you took. Think of the colors that you associate with that time and place. Pull out some scraps and create a palette inspired by your favorite place.

- Pick one of your favorite photos. It could be of your kids, from a vacation, or of a beautiful scenic view. Pull out some scraps based on your photo and create a palette. Look for subtle colors in the details and see how those colors add to the overall color scheme.

- Look at advertisements or product labels. They often have interesting designs and dynamic color schemes that could spark an idea for a quilt. Keep your eyes open. Inspiration really is everywhere.

- Use one of your favorite fabrics as a starting point. Choose colors from that piece of fabric and pull out a bunch of scraps based on those colors. (Refer to the registration dots on the selvage if you get stuck.) Incorporate the inspiration fabric somewhere in the quilt. If you don't use it in the quilt top, use it as the backing or binding to tie the whole thing together.

Paying Attention to Value

Color is just one element in fabric selection. Value (how light or dark a fabric is) is just as important.

Light pink fabrics

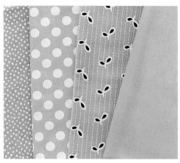

Medium pink fabrics

Dark pink fabrics

Keep in mind that value of a fabric will change depending on the fabrics that are placed next to it. When fabric shopping, a lot of people tend to select fabric in medium values by default. Personally, I gravitate to light- and medium-value fabrics but have very few dark-value fabrics. Look in your stash and make an overall assessment to see what is most prominent in your fabric collection. Do you see a lot of lights? Mediums? Darks? If you notice that you tend to gravitate to one value over the others, try to fill those gaps the next time you are fabric shopping.

Some of my stash

You Don't Need to Use It All

Editing is so important, and I think it is a topic that often gets overlooked in quiltmaking. I am not trying to be contrary when I say that you don't need to use it all. I enjoy using as many scraps as I can, and if I can work some ugly scraps into a piece *and actually make them look good*, so much the better. I always feel a huge sense of accomplishment when I can make that happen. On the other hand, there are times when you simply don't want to use certain scraps. It could be because you have used that same fabric countless times before. It could be that you never really liked the fabric in the first place. It could be for a number of other reasons. If you keep passing over a scrap (and if you are getting tired of seeing it) I encourage you to designate a donation bag and toss it in there. If you really don't like the fabric, don't use it. No need to feel guilty about it, either. Pass along those unwanted scraps to someone who will use them. I try to donate fabric to my guild's free table on a regular basis. If the scraps are very unappealing or are too small for your liking, they can be used as pet bed filling.

Context Is Important

Context is so important when it comes to scraps. The context of a fabric can make or break it—everything depends on the fabrics that are surrounding it.

A few years ago, I learned this lesson while I was teaching a fabric selection class. I had the students select several different fabric combinations from a large scrap pile in the middle of the table. In the scrap pile, there was an unattractive solid butterscotch-colored fabric. It was a fabric that I would have passed over time and time again. In fact, I would have bet money that no one would use it all day long. I thought it would be a good contender for the trash can. One of my students, however, had pulled a few different fabrics, including a colorful batik. The addition of that butterscotch fabric was the one thing that tied the student's whole fabric pull together. It was amazing how that one ugly fabric was transformed after being placed in good company.

Taking Your Time

None of the quilts in this book are weekend projects. Please don't let that intimidate you or stop you from jumping in. You could think of it along the lines of settling in with a good book. These quilts are definitely a labor of love.

Due to the intensity of these quilts, I've found it helpful to work on a few (or more) different projects at a time, staggering the piecing over a period of days, weeks, months, or even years. You could prepare a bunch of pieces to chain piece ahead of time or switch things up between cutting and sewing to prevent fatigue.

You probably don't want to piece several intense quilts back to back. Try to intersperse a few smaller or easier-to-accomplish projects between larger scrap quilts with their more intense piecing.

Finding Time for Smaller Steps

I find it helpful (especially when chain piecing small blocks) to keep my blocks in a basket near my sewing machine. After the blocks are pressed, I set them aside, along with a ruler, a rotary cutter, and a small cutting mat. When I find extra time during the day, the blocks are ready to go, and I can cut a few here and there. It's nice to break up the monotony of trimming blocks into several segments rather than trimming them all at once. It's easier on the arms, too.

Basket of blocks ready to trim

What to Do When Things Aren't Working

Not every quilt turns out to be stellar—even if you have years of experience. The important part is to learn what you can along the way.

My first version of *Scrap Happy Rails* (page 74) started off with an orange, yellow, green, teal, and brown color scheme.

Scrap Happy Rails original color scheme

I added the brown sparingly at first, but as I worked, I kept adding more. Before I knew it, the brown was overpowering the quilt. I realized that I had a quilt that was reminiscent of a 1970s sofa, which was most certainly *not* the look I was going for. I had to stop, assess the situation, and do some editing.

Part of the problem was the color (brown), but it was also the value (too dark). I tried to subtract the brown and add magenta, which didn't work. I auditioned gray in place of the brown, which didn't work either.

In the end I ripped out all the brown strips and decided not to add another color. The results after editing were better.

Somewhere along the way, I realized that the quilt was very reminiscent of a shirt I wore when I was a child. My husband dubbed it "That 70s Shirt," which makes me laugh, and somehow the name makes the quilt better. While it's not my favorite quilt of those I've

made, I can appreciate the things I learned along the way while making it. It's found a home on the back of my couch, and, oddly enough, it matches all of the throw pillows.

Later I remade the quilt in a completely different color scheme, which I like so much better! (See *Scrap Happy Rails*, page 74.)

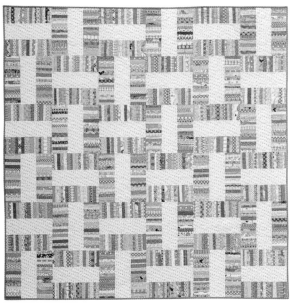

Scrap Happy Rails, version 1, by Amanda Jean Nyberg, quilted by Steffani K. Burton

SUBTLE—THE BEGINNING

Subtle (page 48) started off with the idea of making an Irish Chain quilt, but one using different low-volume backgrounds with various colors for the chain to make it super scrappy. The Irish Chain design depends on significant contrast between the chain blocks and the background fabric. My first attempts at this were unsuccessful. ("Chaotic" would be a better description.) Although my early attempts were less than stellar, I knew my idea had potential and I didn't want to abandon it altogether.

One option for fixing the lack of contrast would be to remove the light patchwork blocks and replace them with one solid or several light-colored prints. I didn't choose this route because it would take away a lot of the scrappy factor, and it would require 6½″ filler blocks rather than 2½″ scrappy squares. The results wouldn't be scrappy enough for my liking.

Another option would be to replace the colored fabrics in each chain block with fabrics of significantly darker value so that the chain design would be distinct. This would have been a good option, but my scrap boxes do not contain nearly enough dark-value fabrics, so I would have had to go fabric shopping or trade scraps with friends.

Subtle—the beginning

Replace light patchwork blocks with 6½″ light squares.

Replace colored fabrics in chain blocks with fabrics of darker value.

Yet another option for fixing the contrast problem would be to make each of the light blocks even lighter. Again, this wasn't an option that would be feasible working from my scrap boxes. I did not have a wide enough variety of light fabrics to make this happen.

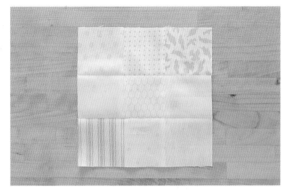

Replace light fabrics in chain blocks with even lighter fabrics.

I spent a few months pondering a solution to this fabric selection problem. One day it hit me: red-and-white polka dots were the answer. They are my favorite, so *of course* they were the answer. By limiting the chain to just one color—and, more important, a consistent value—I made the design more pronounced. This solution created the beautiful but still somewhat subtle design that I was after. I could not be happier with the results. Editing and working through the value and contrast issues made such a difference!

Subtle—the solution

Using Up the Pieces—Alternate Project Ideas

I love to make scrap projects of all sizes, from pincushions to quilts, but there are so many projects that fall in between those two categories. Below are some projects to make if you lose steam but still want to finish (and use) what you've started.

If you only have a few blocks, you could turn them into pot holders, as I did with these Churn Dash blocks. These blocks were the jumping-off point for *Ring Me* (page 102). I tried making blocks with different corner triangle options and then different-colored background fabrics, but I didn't love any of them. I abandoned these blocks and chose to make scrappy squares instead. At 8½" square, the abandoned blocks were perfect for turning into pot holders. I knew I would much rather have usable finished objects than orphan blocks languishing in my sewing room.

My first version of the Chain of Diamonds design was a throw pillow. I had the design idea, but I wasn't very deep into the piecing when I realized I didn't want to tackle a large quilt at that time. The throw pillow, at 16" square, was easy to complete within a reasonable time frame. Since then I have made a larger version (see *Chain of Diamonds*, page 88), but making a throw pillow was a good option for testing out the idea.

After piecing *All Sizes* (page 54), I became smitten with the tiny scale of the smallest half-square triangles that were used in the top section. I had several extra blocks left after making the quilt, so I made more half-square triangles and turned the blocks and the half-square triangles into a quilted cover for a microwavable foot-warmer pack.

Use leftover patchwork pieces and parts for zip pouches, purses, mini quilts, needle books, drawstring bags, storage boxes, fabric buckets, or anything else you can dream up. The sky is the limit!

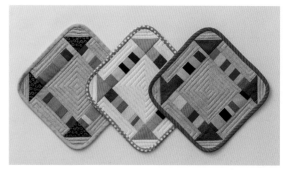

Churn Dash pot holders

Chain of Diamonds pillow

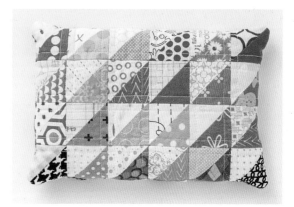

Half-square triangle foot warmer

THE
Flip Side

I love two-sided quilts. Making pieced backs presents a wonderful opportunity to use even more scraps. The front of a quilt is just the beginning; when you turn it over, the back can be a pleasant surprise—another quilt entirely. It's a place where you can let loose and get even more creative. Also, making a two-sided quilt is a great way to stretch your batting dollar.

I like to think of the back side of the quilt as an empty canvas. When it comes time to make a backing, I assess the leftover pieces and parts that were not used on the front and see how I can fit them together, with the addition of any stash fabrics I have on hand. This can be a great place to incorporate leftover or test blocks. On several occasions, I found that I liked the back of my quilt equally as well as (or sometimes even better than) the front of my quilt.

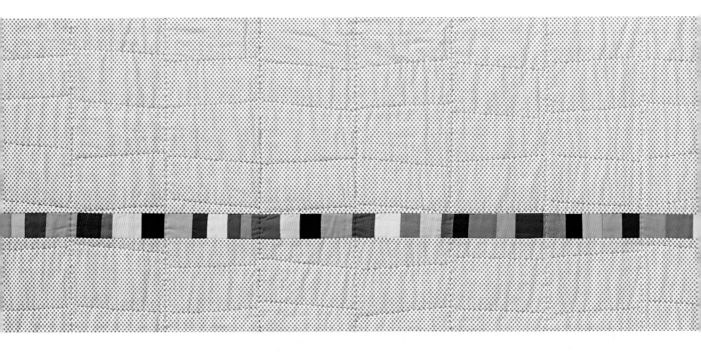

Scrap Options

The following quilts are not included as projects in this book, except for Slopes, Subtle, *and* Donuts (The Size of Your Head).

In the Middle produced lots of scraps, so I pieced them into half-rectangle blocks. The patchwork row between the two solid fabrics creates a striking quilt back.

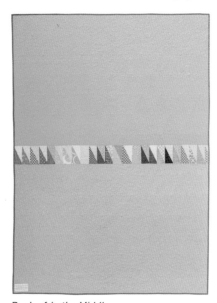

In the Middle by Amanda Jean Nyberg

Back of *In the Middle*

The front of *Ladder Leap* was strip pieced. I cut the leftover parts to a suitable height and filled in the space needed using the extras. I was able to reduce the purchased backing needed from 5½ yards down to 4¼ yards simply by adding the scrap strip.

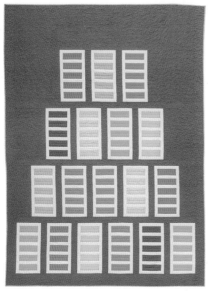

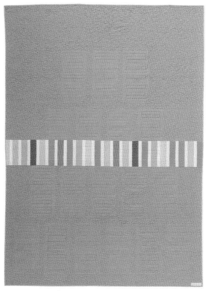

Ladder Leap by Amanda Jean Nyberg

Back of *Ladder Leap*

Stash Options

When it comes to lap quilts, using eight half-yard cuts is one of my favorite backing solutions. The piecing is fairly simple, and it produces an interesting quilt back. This is a great way to mix and match some favorite prints from your stash rather than purchase additional yardage.

Café Umbrellas by Amanda Jean Nyberg

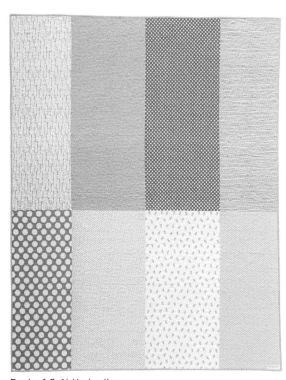

Back of *Café Umbrellas*

The backing for *Math Facts* was designed around the orange scissors fabric. It was a perfect match for the front of the quilt, and I wanted to use it on the back somehow, but I only had a quarter yard of it. I found two other orange fabrics, cut them to approximately the same size as the scissors fabric, and floated all three pieces on a solid cream background. This is one of my favorite pieced quilt backs. It's a great way to highlight a small amount of a favorite fabric.

Math Facts by Amanda Jean Nyberg

Back of *Math Facts*

This polka dot print would be nearly impossible to piece together without an obvious seam that would catch your eye every time you looked at it. The addition of the patchwork strip is a good solution. There is no need to worry about how the print of the fabric will line up, and it is a great opportunity to use up some of the leftovers from the front.

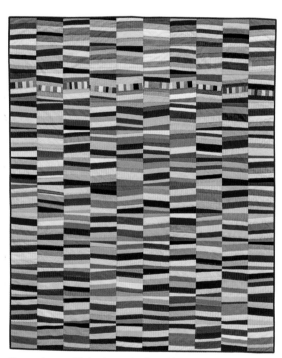

Slopes (page 62) by Amanda Jean Nyberg

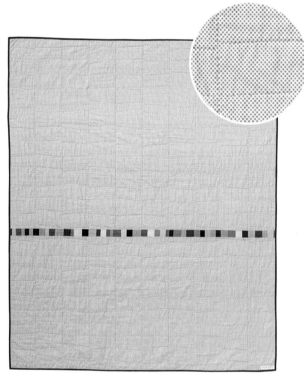

Back of *Slopes*

The backing of *A Squared* is a great example of how to make a piece of fabric that may be too small stretch a little further. I had about a yard and a half of this fun summertime print. It complemented the front of the quilt, but I certainly didn't have enough to cover the back. The solution was to add a large chunky border in a solid color. This framed layout draws more attention to the print than if the whole backing were covered with the one fabric. This is a great way to showcase a large-scale or novelty print.

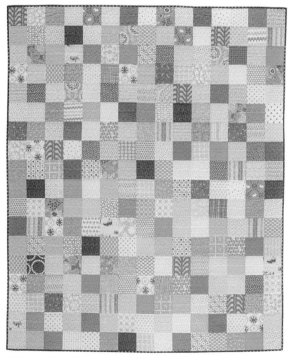

A Squared by Amanda Jean Nyberg

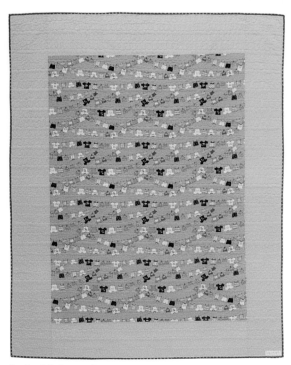

Back of *A Squared*

The back of *Subtle* also uses a strip of patchwork to break up the polka dot print, as well as leftover squares from the front. The line of patchwork runs vertically rather than horizontally, but either way works beautifully. It has the most pleasing effect if the strip is offset using the rule of thirds (meaning that the strip of patchwork doesn't slice directly through the middle of the fabric but instead is placed about a third of the way from the edge, leaving two-thirds of the backing on the other side of the patchwork).

Subtle (page 48) by Amanda Jean Nyberg

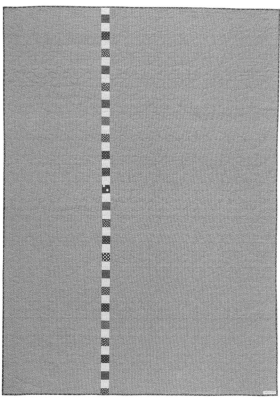

Back of *Subtle*

Using Orphan or Test Blocks

I made *Bruce's Quilt* for my brother a few years ago. Rather than follow a pattern, I chose to make up my own block measurements. It took me a few tries to get the measurements just right, so I had three leftover quilt blocks after the top was pieced. Incorporating the test blocks into the backing adds a lot of interest, and the bonus is that I have three fewer orphan blocks hanging around in my sewing room!

Bruce's Quilt by Amanda Jean Nyberg

Back of *Bruce's Quilt*

The back of *Donuts (The Size of Your Head)* also uses up orphan blocks. The blocks were from another project entirely, but I had several of them left over. They were a perfect match for the quilt front, both in color and in shape, so I incorporated them into the backing. I didn't want the blocks to run off the sides of the quilt, so I added a filler fabric on either side of the blocks to prevent this from happening.

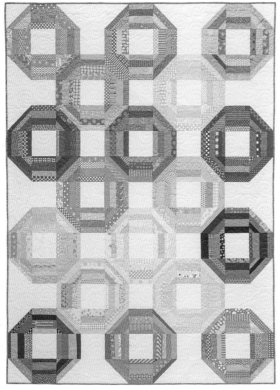

Donuts (The Size of Your Head) (page 68) by Amanda Jean Nyberg

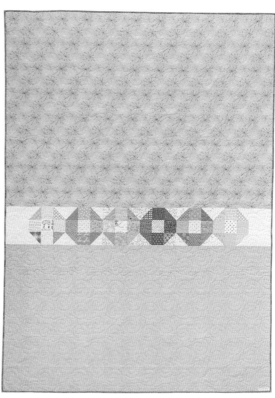

Back of *Donuts (The Size of Your Head)*

PROJECTS USING
Squares

Mini Nines

Finished block: 3½″ × 3½″   •   Finished quilt: 59½″ × 70″

When I first started making this quilt, I cut individual 1″ × 1″ squares and sewed them together to make the Nine-Patches. Thankfully a friend suggested that I use strip-piecing methods to make the Nine-Patch blocks in order to speed up the process. At first I was hesitant to do so, but after making a few blocks, I knew it was the only way to go. My speed dramatically increased *and* my piecing accuracy improved.

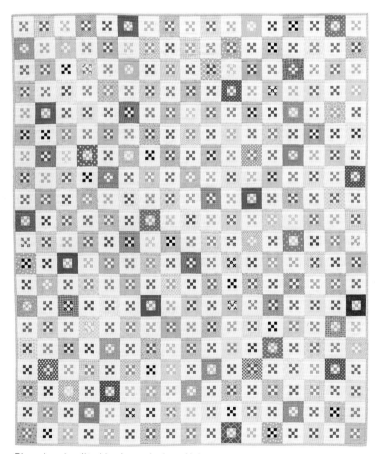

Pieced and quilted by Amanda Jean Nyberg

Tiny Piecing

Tiny piecing can be frustrating, especially if you aren't an extremely accurate sewist. (I know I fit into that category.) Before cutting out all of the pieces for this quilt, I highly recommend that you make a few test blocks following the tips below and that you test the accuracy of your seam allowance (see Testing Your Seam Allowance, page 39).

If you're still having difficulties, you may want to consider cutting the block border pieces a little larger than the instructions state to give yourself some wiggle room. (Adjust according to your personal preference.) If you choose to make the blocks oversized, trim each block down to 4″ × 4″ (unfinished) after piecing.

Other tips for accuracy:

• Cutting accurately is very important. If your pieces aren't cut correctly, an accurate seam allowance is a moot point. Every inaccuracy will continue to cause problems (and perhaps be magnified) as you progress through your project.

• Use the same sewing machine for piecing the entire quilt top.

• Use a thin (50wt) thread for piecing. Thicker thread will shrink your seam allowance.

• Press—don't iron. Press carefully! It does make a difference.

Materials

A variety of small-scale prints and solids: 68 strips 1″ × 27″ for the Nine-Patch centers, and 170 strips 1½″ × 12½″ for the block borders

White: 3½ yards

Backing: 4 yards

Binding: ⅝ yard

Cotton batting: 68″ × 78″

Cutting

WOF = width of fabric

SMALL-SCALE PRINTS AND SOLIDS

Nine-Patch centers

From each of the 68 strips, cut:

  1 piece 1″ × 5½″

  2 pieces 1″ × 10½″

Keep the sets of pieces cut from the same fabric together.

Block borders

From each of the 170 strips, cut:

  2 pieces 1½″ × 2″

  2 pieces 1½″ × 4″

Keep the sets of pieces cut from the same fabric together.

WHITE

Nine-Patch centers

Cut 40 strips 1″ × WOF.

  Subcut:

  68 pieces 1″ × 10½″

  136 pieces 1″ × 5½″

Block borders

Cut 51 strips 1½″ × WOF.

  Subcut:

  340 pieces 1½″ × 2″

  340 pieces 1½″ × 4″

BINDING

Cut 8 strips 2½″ × WOF.

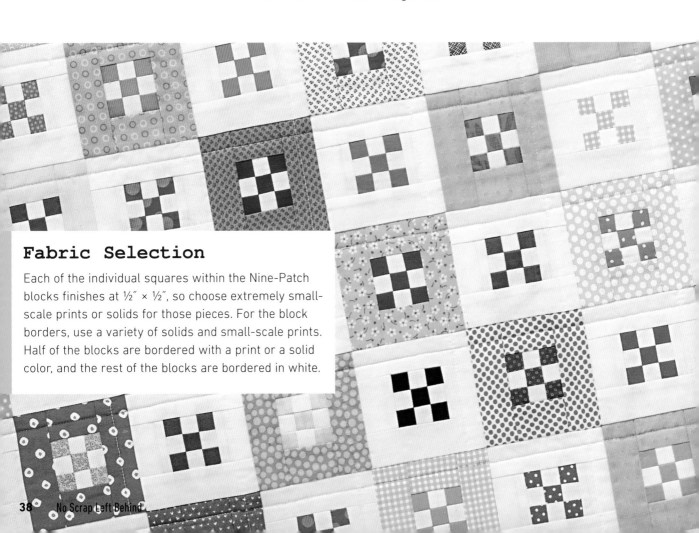

Fabric Selection

Each of the individual squares within the Nine-Patch blocks finishes at ½″ × ½″, so choose extremely small-scale prints or solids for those pieces. For the block borders, use a variety of solids and small-scale prints. Half of the blocks are bordered with a print or a solid color, and the rest of the blocks are bordered in white.

Testing Your Seam Allowance

To test the accuracy of your seam allowance, follow these steps:

1. Cut 2 fabric pieces 2½″ × 4½″.

2. Sew together with a ¼″ seam.

3. Carefully press the seam to one side or open.

4. Measure the piece. It should be exactly 4½″ × 4½″ square.

   • If the piece is less than 4½″ across, your seam allowance is too large and should be adjusted accordingly.

   • If the piece is larger than 4½″ across, your seam allowance is too scant and should be adjusted accordingly.

5. Make the necessary adjustments and start over from the beginning, until you have achieved an exact ¼″ seam allowance.

6. Once you achieve an exact ¼″, mark that spot on your sewing machine. This can be done with painter's tape or a metal seam guide. Since both guide options are temporary, you may want to sew through the edge of an index card with a ¼″ seam. Keep that index card for future reference. When you need to re-mark that exact spot on your sewing machine, place the needle down through a stitched hole, then place tape along the edge of the index card. This should yield an accurate ¼″ seam allowance time and time again.

Construction

All seam allowances are ¼″ unless otherwise noted. Use a smaller stitch length for the strip sets to avoid seams opening up after subcutting.

1. Arrange 2 colored 1″ × 10½″ pieces and 1 white 1″ × 10½″ piece. Sew the pieces together. Press the seams open. Cut the strip set into 1″ segments. Each strip set will yield 10 pieces. **Fig. A**

A

B

2. Arrange 2 white 1″ × 5½″ pieces and 1 colored 1″ × 5½″ piece. Sew the pieces together. Press the seams open. Cut the strip set into 1″ segments. Each strip set will yield 5 pieces. **Fig. B**

C

3. Arrange 2 segments from Step 1 and 1 segment from Step 2, as shown, to create a checkerboard pattern. **Fig. C**

D

4. Sew 3 rows together to make 1 Nine-Patch center. Press the seams open. Repeat to make a total of 5 Nine-Patch centers. **Fig. D**

5. Repeat Steps 1–4 with the remaining 67 fabrics to make a total of 340 Nine-Patch centers.

6. Arrange a Nine-Patch center and 4 border pieces. **Fig. E**

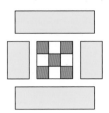

E

F

G

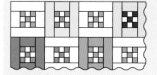
7. Sew the 1½˝ × 2˝ border pieces to the left and the right of the Nine-Patch block. Press the seams toward the outside.

8. Sew the 1½˝ × 4˝ border pieces to the top and bottom of the block. Press the seams toward the outside. **Fig. F**

9. Repeat Steps 6–8 to border a total of 170 blocks with small-scale or solid-colored fabrics.

10. Repeat Steps 6–8 to border the remaining 170 blocks with white fabric. **Fig. G**

11. Arrange the blocks according to the quilt assembly diagram.

12. Sew the blocks into rows. Press. Sew the rows together to complete the quilt top. Press the quilt top well.

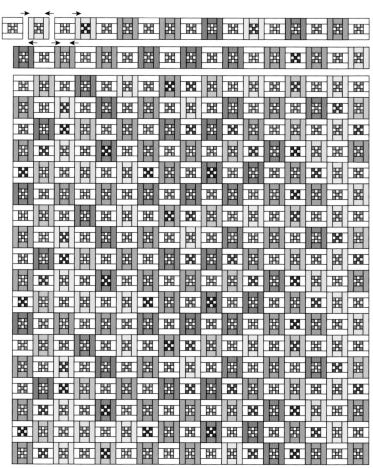

Quilt assembly

FINISHING

1. Sew around the perimeter of the quilt top ⅛″ from the edge. This will prevent the seams from splitting during handling before it is quilted.

2. Piece the back to measure at least 68″ × 78″.

3. Baste, quilt, and bind, using your preferred methods. Label if you wish.

4. Wash and dry.

About the Backing

I worked on this quilt sporadically, so it took me about two and a half years to piece it. After that long journey, I knew I had to put the word *perseverance* on the back. I planned to paper piece the letters, but I ran out of time, so I quilted the word and pieced that into the backing instead.

Hot & Cold

Finished block: 2″ × 2   •   Finished quilt: 62″ × 76″

Although I would be hard-pressed to pick a favorite quilt from this book, this one would have to be near the top of the list. This quilt exemplifies how simple yet beautiful a scrap quilt can be. It certainly doesn't have to be complicated. This quilt is made from humble squares (in solids, no less!), and it is a great way to play with color. Separating the warm colors from the cool colors, then arranging those two groups separately, is a fun twist on color blocking. Feel free to change up the size and shape of the warm color sections if you wish.

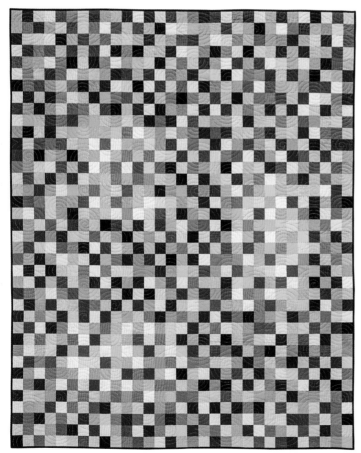

Pieced by Amanda Jean Nyberg; quilted by Steffani K. Burton

Materials

Solid scraps in a variety of cool colors (greens, blues, purples) and values: about 4½ yards total

Solid scraps in a variety of warm colors (pinks, reds, oranges, yellows) and values: about 1 yard total

Backing: 4⅞ yards

Binding: ⅝ yard

Cotton batting: 70″ × 84″

Cutting

WOF = width of fabric

SOLIDS:

Cut 975 squares 2½″ × 2½″ from cool-colored scraps.

Cut 203 squares 2½″ × 2½″ from warm-colored scraps.

BINDING

Cut 8 strips 2½″ × WOF.

Tip

Cut Extra Squares

You may want to cut several more squares than the pattern calls for, which will allow flexibility during the layout process. The total needed for a 31 by 38 square layout as shown is 1,178 squares.

Make It Faster

If you prefer a quicker method, you can strip piece some of the blocks together rather than cutting out individual squares. To do this, cut your fabric into 2½″-wide strips instead of individual squares. Piece the long sides of the strips together in sets of two, three, or four. Press the seams to one side, and then cut into 2½″ segments. Use a combination of strip-pieced and individually cut blocks, and follow the quilt assembly diagram as directed (page 47). Some of the seams may need to be pressed in a different direction during assembly, so take that into consideration when using this method.

Fabric Selection

Solid fabrics from several manufacturers were used in this quilt. An alternative would be to sew it up in a variety of prints, which would dramatically change the look. Use a complete range of values (lights, mediums, and darks) to produce the pixelated effect.

Construction

All seam allowances are ¼″ unless otherwise noted.

1. Arrange the squares on a design wall in a 31 by 38 square layout according to the quilt assembly diagram (next page). Take photos with a digital camera to gauge your progress. Make sure that the colors and values are evenly distributed throughout the quilt. Take a digital photo of the final arrangement to refer to during assembly.

2. Sew the squares into rows. Press the seams, following the quilt assembly diagram.

About the Process

While I was working on the layout of this quilt, I took at least 44 progress shots with my camera. I finalized the entire arrangement before sewing any of the blocks together because I wanted to make sure that the color and value balance was just right.

Tip

Keeping Blocks in Order

To keep blocks (or squares) in order between the design wall and the sewing machine, work on one row at a time. Pick up the blocks from left to right. Each time you pick up a new block, place it beneath the previous block. Take the blocks to the sewing machine and chain piece pairs of blocks together. Snip the threads between the blocks apart and place them in the order that they were sewn, from left to right. Sew those pairs together. Repeat this until all the blocks are sewn into one strip.

3. Sew the rows together according to the quilt assembly diagram. Press well.

Tip

Pin for Accuracy

When sewing the rows together, pin at each intersection to achieve crisp, accurate results.

FINISHING

1. Sew around the perimeter of the quilt top ⅛″ from the edge. This will prevent the seams from splitting during handling before it is quilted.

2. Piece the back to measure at least 70″ × 84″.

3. Baste, quilt, and bind, using your preferred methods. Label if you wish.

4. Wash and dry.

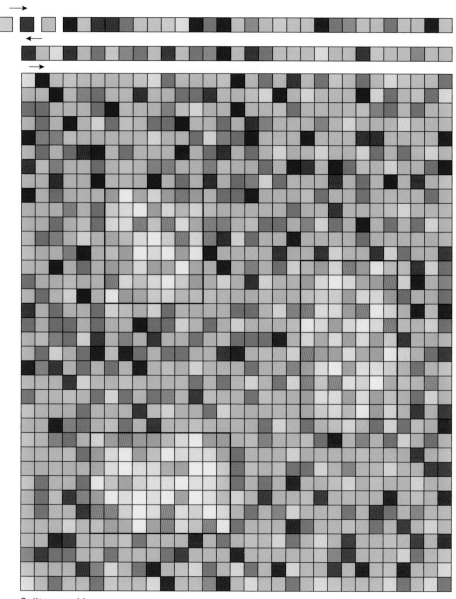

Quilt assembly

Subtle

Finished block: 6″ × 6″ • Finished quilt: 66″ × 90″

This quilt began as a multicolored Irish Chain, but there wasn't enough contrast between the chain and the background blocks, and so the design didn't show up as well as I had hoped. By limiting the color of the chain to just one color—and more important, a consistent value—the design became more pronounced. The variety of background fabrics produces a vintage feel that I absolutely love.

Pieced by Amanda Jean Nyberg; quilted by Steffani K. Burton

Materials

Light-colored scraps in a variety of prints and solids: 5 yards total

Various red-and-white polka-dot fabrics: 2¼ yards total

Backing: 5⅝ yards

Binding: ¾ yard

Cotton batting: 74″ × 98″

Cutting

WOF = width of fabric

LIGHT-COLORED SCRAPS
Cut 1,070 squares 2½″ × 2½″.

RED-AND-WHITE POLKA-DOT FABRICS
Cut 415 squares 2½″ × 2½″.

BINDING
Cut 9 strips 2½″ × WOF.

Make It Faster

If you would rather make this quilt from your stash or if you have larger fabric scraps, you may want to strip piece some or all of the blocks. To do this, cut your fabric into 2½″ strips instead of individual squares. Piece the long sides of the strips together in sets of two or three, press, and then cut into 2½″ segments. Assemble the blocks as indicated in Construction (page 52).

Fabric Selection

Several light-colored fabric scraps were used for the background. A variety of red-and-white polka-dot fabrics were used for the chain. If you are unsure of your fabric choices, audition them on a design wall. Step back several feet to determine if the combination is successful or not. This is especially helpful when determining if a particular background fabric will blend with the others or if it will stand out too much.

Construction

All seam allowances are ¼″ unless otherwise noted.

1. Select 9 light 2½″ × 2½″ squares and arrange them in a 3 × 3 grid. Sew the blocks together into 3 rows. Press the seams open. Sew 3 rows together to make 1 block. Press the seams open. Repeat this step to make a total of 82 light blocks.

2. Select 5 red-and-white 2½″ × 2½″′ squares and 4 light 2½″ × 2½″ squares. Arrange blocks in a 3 × 3 grid. Sew the blocks together into 3 rows. Press the seams open. Sew 3 rows together to make 1 block. Press the seams open. Repeat to make a total of 83 red-and-white blocks.

3. Arrange the blocks in a pleasing manner, alternating the light and the red-and-white blocks. Use the quilt assembly diagram (next page) as a guide. Sew the blocks into rows. Press the seams open.

4. Sew the rows together to complete the quilt top. Press the quilt top well.

FINISHING

1. Sew around the perimeter of the quilt top ⅛″ from the edge. This will prevent the seams from splitting during handling before it is quilted.

2. Piece the back to measure at least 74″ × 98″.

3. Baste, quilt, and bind, using your preferred methods. Label if you wish.

4. Wash and dry.

Tip

Pressing Seams

I pressed the seams open when making the blocks for my quilt, which prevented the red fabric from shadowing through the light fabrics. If you prefer to press your seams to the side, follow the arrows for pressing directions.

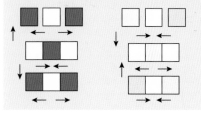

Quilt assembly

All Sizes

Finished blocks: 1½″ × 1½″, 2″ × 2″, 3″ × 3″, 4″ × 4″, 5″ × 5″
Finished quilt: 60″ × 77½″

This quilt was inspired by clothing tag sizes—small, medium, and large (S, M, L). I decided to expand the idea by adding extra-small (XS) triangles, which are a great way to use mini charm squares, and extra-large (XL) triangles, which are great for using more scraps faster.

Pieced by Amanda Jean Nyberg; quilted by Steffani K. Burton

Materials

Scraps in a variety of light fabrics:
about 3¼ yards total

Scraps in a variety of dark fabrics:
about 3¼ yards total

Backing: 5 yards

Binding: ⅝ yard

Cotton batting: 68″ × 86″

Cutting:

WOF = width of fabric

Size of square	Number of lights needed	Number of darks needed
XL: 6″ × 6″	30	30
L: 5″ × 5″	38	38
M: 4″ × 4″	50	50
S: 3″ × 3″	75	75
XS: 2½″ × 2½″	100	100

BINDING

Cut 8 strips 2½″ × WOF.

Fabric Selection

For each block, select pairs of fabrics that have a significant amount of contrast. If you are unsure of a fabric combination, place the two fabrics next to each other on a design wall and step back about ten feet. Viewing the pair of fabrics from a distance will help you determine if the combination is successful or not. It is helpful to place the finished blocks on a design wall as you make them so you can assess the contrast and color balance throughout the entire piecing process.

If you have triangles from previous projects (trimmings from constructing other quilt blocks, leftovers from making bias binding, and so on) and the sizes are appropriate, consider sewing them together to make blocks for this quilt.

Construction

All seam allowances are ¼″ unless otherwise noted.

1. Consult Basic Half-Square Triangle Block Construction (next page) to make half-square triangle (HST) blocks in the following sizes:

Starting size of squares	Number of pairs needed	Trim size	Total HST blocks
XL: 6″ × 6″	30	5½″ × 5½″	60
L: 5″ × 5″	38	4½″ × 4½″	76*
M: 4″ × 4″	50	3½″ × 3½″	100
S: 3″ × 3″	75	2½″ × 2½″	150
XS: 2½″ × 2½″	100	2″ × 2″	200

There will be 1 extra HST block in this size after the layout is complete.

2. Arrange the HST blocks in a pleasing manner using the table below and the quilt assembly diagram (page 60) as a guide. Sew the blocks into 5 rows of each size, and follow the arrows for pressing directions. Sew the rows together to complete the quilt top. Press the quilt top well.

HST size	HST blocks per row
XL	12
L	15
M	20
S	30
XS	40

NOTE: About Construction

An accurate ¼″ seam allowance is very important in this quilt. If your seam allowance is off by even a little bit, that measurement will add up across the width of the quilt, and the sections will not align properly when you sew them together. To prevent this from happening, measure each row after assembly. The rows should measure exactly 60½″ wide. Press carefully, and pin at each intersection to improve accuracy and maintain the triangle points. This is one quilt in particular where sewing with a scant ¼″ seam allowance will help maintain accuracy. Refer to Testing Your Seam Allowance (page 39) to test and set your seam allowance.

Basic Half-Square Triangle Block Construction

1. Select 2 squares of equal size, 1 light and 1 dark. Place the squares right sides together. **Fig. A**

2. Use a sharp pencil to draw a diagonal line on the back of the light-colored square. **Fig. B**

3. Sew on both sides of the line, using a ¼″ seam allowance. **Fig. C**

4. Cut on the pencil line. **Fig. D**

5. Press the seams open or toward the darker fabric, whichever you prefer. **Fig. E**

6. Trim the block. For example, if you start with a large 5″ × 5″ square, trim the block down to 4½″ × 4½″, which will yield a 4″ finished half-square triangle block. Follow the directions in the trimming table (previous page) for specific cutting and trimming sizes. Each pair of squares will yield 2 half-square triangle blocks. **Fig. F**

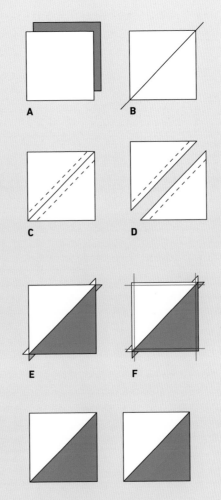

Note: There are many ways to make a half-square triangle (HST) block, but the method above seems to be the easiest and the most straightforward one I have found. Trimming down the blocks after piecing is an extra step, but I find that it yields the most accurate results. If you prefer a different half-square triangle construction method, by all means use it. If you choose a different construction method, be sure to adjust the cutting sizes as needed.

FINISHING

1. Sew around the perimeter of the quilt top ⅛″ from the edge. This will prevent the seams from splitting during handling before it is quilted.

2. Piece the back to measure at least 68″ × 86″.

3. Baste, quilt, and bind, using your preferred methods. Label if you wish.

4. Wash and dry.

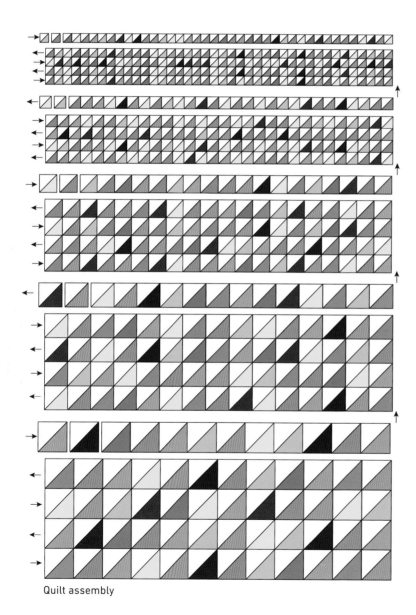

Quilt assembly

PROJECTS USING
Strips and Strings

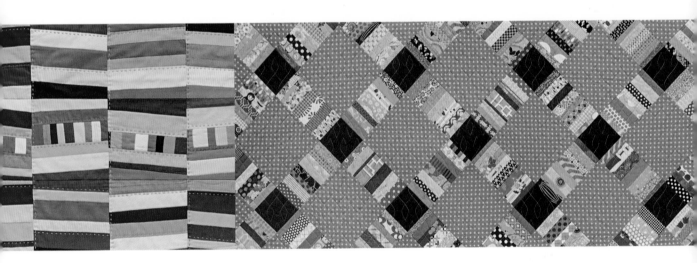

Slopes

Finished block: 6″ × 6″   •   Finished quilt: 60″ × 72″

The motivation to make this quilt was plain and simple: my solid scrap bin (a cube that measures 13″ on each side) was full. That's a lot of scraps! Apparently I've used quite a few solids in projects over the years. After piecing this quilt top, I'm happy to report that the bin is now only half full, and I used nearly all of my green scraps. It's good to see progress.

After making several string blocks, I had a bunch of little bits left over. I decided to piece them together to make scrappy strings, which I incorporated into some of the blocks. I included one row of these ultra-scrappy blocks across the width of the quilt, but you could add more if you like.

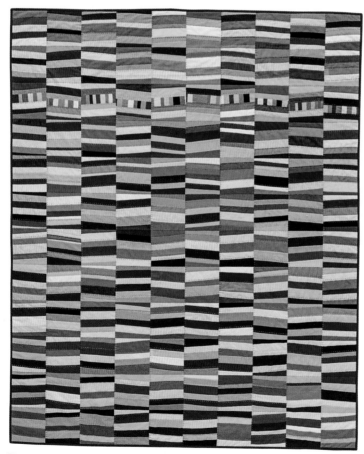

Pieced and quilted by Amanda Jean Nyberg

Materials

Solid scraps in a variety of colors and values: about 6½ yards total

Backing: 4 yards

Binding: ⅝ yard

Cotton batting: 68″ × 80″

6½″ × 6½″ square quilting ruler

Cutting

WOF = width of fabric

SOLIDS

Cut (or collect) 720–750 strings of fabric measuring 1″–2″ wide and about 7″ long.

BINDING

Cut 8 strips 2½″ × WOF.

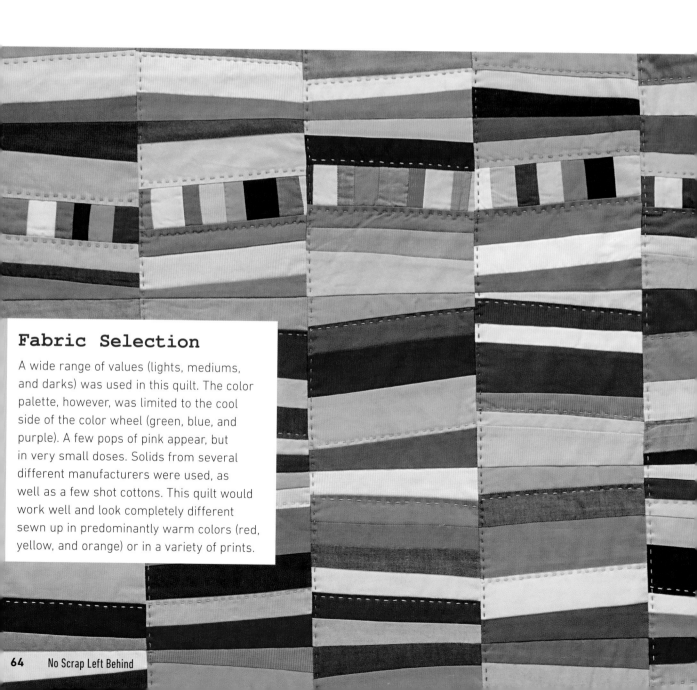

Fabric Selection

A wide range of values (lights, mediums, and darks) was used in this quilt. The color palette, however, was limited to the cool side of the color wheel (green, blue, and purple). A few pops of pink appear, but in very small doses. Solids from several different manufacturers were used, as well as a few shot cottons. This quilt would work well and look completely different sewn up in predominantly warm colors (red, yellow, and orange) or in a variety of prints.

Construction

All seam allowances are ¼″ unless otherwise noted.

1. Sew several strings together side by side until the block is at least 7″ × 7″ square. Press well. Use steam or spray starch to help the block lie flat. Press the seams open or to the side, whichever you prefer. Make 110 blocks. Sewing a few larger blocks is fine, as the trimmed bits can be reused.

> ## Tip
>
> ### Vary the Width of the Strips
>
> The number of strips needed for each block will vary depending on the width of each strip. Use wider strips on the outermost edges of each block to allow plenty of room for trimming.

2. Place the ruler on top of 1 block and tilt the ruler to the right a bit. Trim on all 4 sides so the block measures 6½″ × 6½″ square. Repeat for a total of 55 blocks.

3. Place the ruler on top of 1 block and tilt the ruler to the left a bit. Trim on all 4 sides so the block measures 6½″ × 6½″ square. Repeat for a total of 55 blocks.

4. Sew several of the leftover bits from Steps 2 and 3 end to end until the piece measures about 7″ × 1½″–2″. Repeat this step to make a total of 10 scrappy strips. Press each strip well.

5. Trim each of the scrappy strips anywhere from 1¼″ to 1½″ wide. A variety of widths adds interest, but be sure to trim each strip to a consistent width. (Avoid making wedge-shaped strips.)

6. Sew several solid strings together, incorporating 1 scrappy strip somewhere in the middle of the block, to make a block at least 7″ × 7″ square. Repeat this step to make a total of 10 blocks. Press well.

7. Place the ruler on top of 1 block and tilt the ruler to the right a bit, as shown in Step 2 (at left). Trim on all 4 sides so the block measures 6½″ × 6½″ square. Repeat for a total of 5 blocks.

8. Place the ruler on top of 1 block and tilt the ruler to the left a bit, as shown in Step 3 (page 65). Trim on all 4 sides so the block measures 6½″ × 6½″ square. Repeat for a total of 5 blocks.

9. Using the quilt assembly diagram (next page) as a guide, arrange the blocks in a pleasing manner, alternating the left- and right-leaning blocks from row to row and column to column. Sew the blocks into rows. Follow the arrows for pressing directions. Sew the rows together to complete the quilt top. Press the quilt top well.

FINISHING

1. Sew around the perimeter of the quilt top ⅛″ from the edge. This will prevent the seams from splitting during handling before it is quilted.

2. Piece the back to measure at least 68″ × 80″.

3. Baste, quilt, and bind, using your preferred methods. Label if you wish.

4. Wash and dry.

About the Quilting

Several years ago a friend gave me a boxed set of Anna Maria Horner's beautiful perle cotton as a gift. The threads are fine, the colors are gorgeous, and they are almost too pretty to use. I've used them sparingly over the years, on little projects here and there. When I discovered that the box of threads matched this quilt perfectly, I knew that I needed to use them to finish the quilt—it was meant to be. The hand quilting took extra time and effort, but I found it comforting and relaxing, so it was well worth it. The result was a soft quilt that drapes beautifully. It was an absolute delight to quilt this by hand.

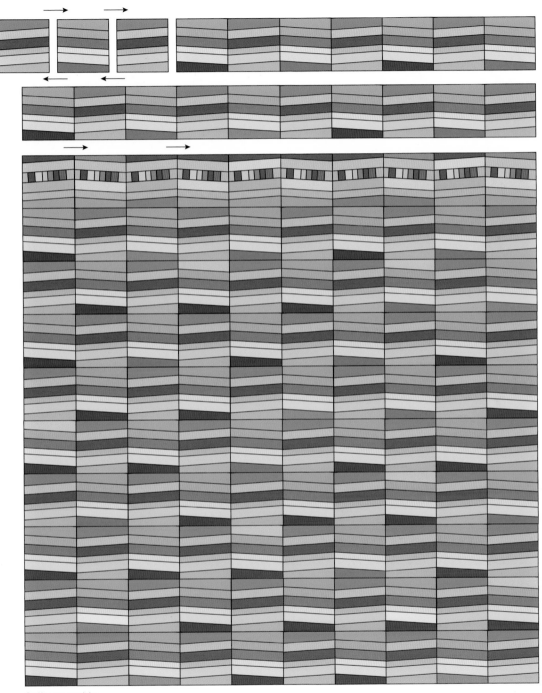

Quilt assembly

Donuts (THE SIZE OF YOUR HEAD)

Finished block: 18″ × 18″   •   Finished quilt: 66″ × 90″

There is a bakery in a small town near my house that sells the most amazing donuts—donuts the size of your head! The large-scale blocks in this quilt remind me of those donuts. The interlocking blocks make this quilt look more complex than it actually is. A design wall is especially helpful when making this quilt, because all of the blocks need to be arranged before you begin sewing the quilt top together.

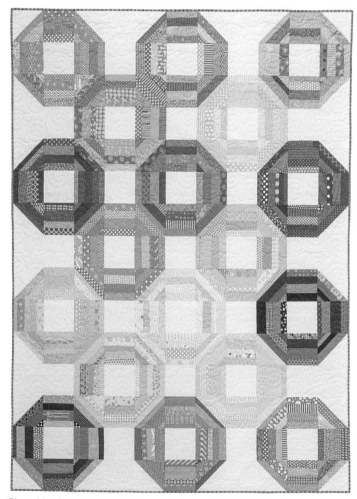

Pieced by Amanda Jean Nyberg; quilted by Steffani K. Burton

Materials

Strips and strings in a variety of colors: about 6 yards total

Background: 2¼ yards

Backing: 5⅝ yards

Binding: ¾ yard

Cotton batting: 74″ × 98″

6½″ Easy Angle quilting ruler (highly recommended) *or* **template plastic**

Optional (but recommended): 6½″ × 6½″ square quilting ruler

Cutting

WOF = width of fabric

STRIPS AND STRINGS

For the squares:

Cut (or collect) approximately 288–360 strings 1½″–2½″ × 7″.

For the triangles:

Cut (or collect) approximately 72 strings 1½″–2½″ × 4½″.

Cut (or collect) approximately 72 strings 1½″–2½″ × 6½″.

Cut (or collect) approximately 72 strings 1½″–2½″ × 10½″.*

*If following Alternative Triangle Construction (next page), you will need approximately 36 strips 3″–4″ × 10½″.

BACKGROUND

Cut 45 squares 6½″ × 6½″.

Cut 12 squares 6⅞″ × 6⅞″.

   Subcut on the diagonal once to create 24 half-square triangles.

BINDING

Cut 9 strips 2½″ × WOF.

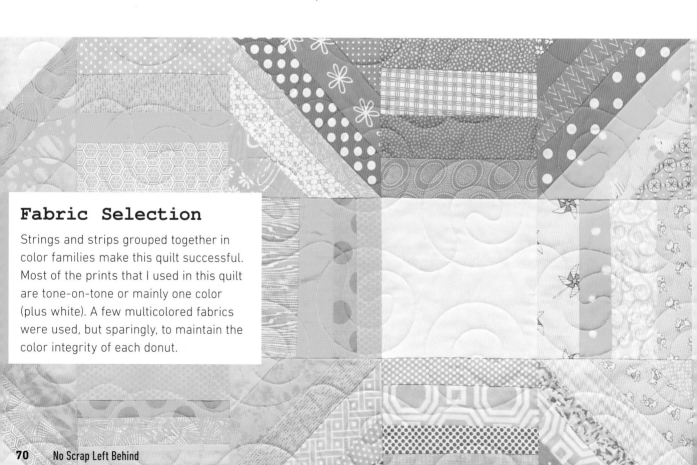

Fabric Selection

Strings and strips grouped together in color families make this quilt successful. Most of the prints that I used in this quilt are tone-on-tone or mainly one color (plus white). A few multicolored fabrics were used, but sparingly, to maintain the color integrity of each donut.

Alternative Triangle Construction

One of the great things about quilting is that there are so many different methods of construction. I used the Easy Angle ruler to make the triangles for my quilt because I had the ruler on hand. The blocks can also be made without the ruler or a template.

1. Start with a 3″–4″ × 10½″ string. This will become the long side of the triangle.

2. Piece shorter strings on either side to make a block at least 7″ × 7″ square.

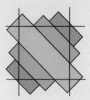

3. Trim the block to 6⅞″ × 6⅞″ square.

4. Cut the square through the center on the diagonal once, parallel to the seamlines, to create 2 half-square triangles.

5. Repeat Steps 1–4 to make 2 string blocks (for a total of 4 half-square triangles) per donut. These blocks will replace the blocks made in Step 3 (at right).

Construction

All seam allowances are ¼″ unless otherwise noted.

1. If you do not have a 6½″ Easy Angle ruler, copy and trace the triangle template (page 73) onto template plastic. Cut it out with sharp scissors. (Thin cardboard or thick card stock could work in place of template plastic, if necessary.) *Or* see Alternative Triangle Construction (at left).

2. Sew strings (7″ long) from the same color family together side by side until the block measures at least 6½″ × 7″. Press the seams open or to the side, whichever you prefer. Use spray starch to help the block lie flat. Trim the block to 6½″ × 6½″. Repeat this step to make a total of 4 blocks in the same color family.

Tip

Vary the Width of the Strips

The number of strips needed for each block will vary depending on the width of each strip. Use wider strips on the outermost edge of each block to allow plenty of room for trimming.

3. Sew strings (4½″, 6½″, and 10½″ long) of the same color family together side by side until the patchwork is larger than the Easy Angle ruler or template. Press the seams to the side. Trim, using the ruler or template as a guide. Repeat this step to make a total of 4 triangles from the same color family.

NOTE:

Blocks from Steps 2 and 3 (page 71) will yield 1 donut when arranged as shown in the quilt assembly diagram (at right).

4. Repeat Steps 2 and 3 to make 18 donuts in a variety of colors.

5. Place the donut block components in a pleasing arrangement on a design wall. Fill in the background pieces of the quilt, using the quilt assembly diagram (at right) as a guide.

6. Sew the pairs of triangles together to make blocks.

7. Sew all the blocks into rows. Follow the arrows for pressing directions. Sew the rows together to complete the quilt top. Press the quilt top well.

FINISHING

1. Sew around the perimeter of the quilt top ⅛″ from the edge. This will prevent the seams from splitting during handling before it is quilted.

2. Piece the back to measure at least 74″ × 98″.

3. Baste, quilt, and bind, using your preferred methods. Label if you wish.

4. Wash and dry.

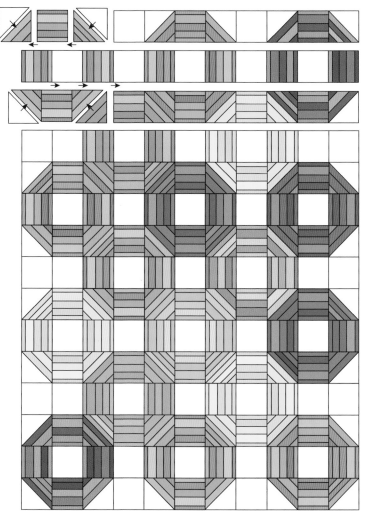

Quilt assembly

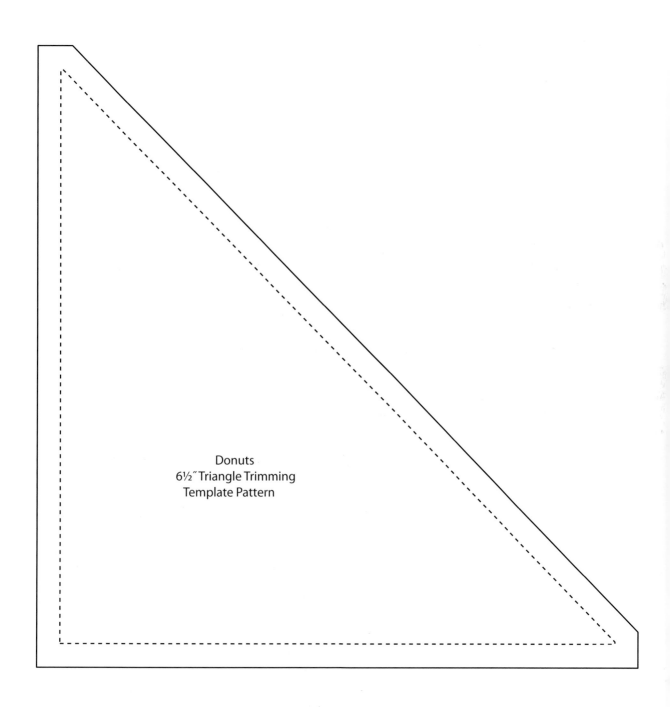

Donuts
6½″ Triangle Trimming
Template Pattern

Scrap Happy Rails

Finished block: 12″ × 12″ • Finished quilt: 72″ × 72″

I love a Rail Fence quilt—you can't beat it for simplicity and easy assembly. I thought it would be fun to make one that was super scrappy, so I started with strings that were about 1¼″–1½″ wide. Charm packs, cut into strips, would work beautifully for this quilt—an easy way to add a large variety of fabrics to a quilt without spending a lot of money.

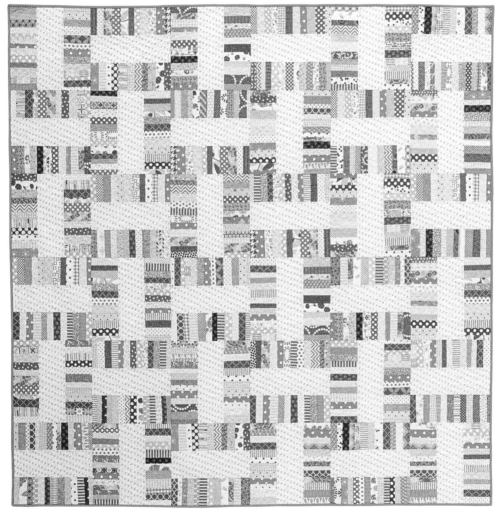

Pieced and quilted by Amanda Jean Nyberg

Materials

**Strips and strings at least
1¼˝ wide:** about 5 yards total

Background: 1⅔ yards

Backing: 4⅝ yards

Binding: ¾ yard

Cotton batting: 80˝ × 80˝

Cutting

WOF = width of fabric

STRIPS AND STRINGS

Cut (or collect) 900–1,000 strings of fabric
that measure 1¼˝–1½˝ × 4¾˝.

BACKGROUND

Cut 12 strips 4½˝ × WOF.

Subcut 36 rectangles 4½˝ × 12½˝.

BINDING

Cut 9 strips 2½˝ × WOF.

Make It Faster

If you prefer a quicker method, this quilt
can be made using strip-piecing methods.
To do this, use strings that are 14˝ long.
Piece them together side by side to make
a strip set that is 12½˝ wide. Press well.
Cut the strip set into 3 pieces 4½˝ × 12½˝.
Distribute the strips that are exactly alike
into different blocks.

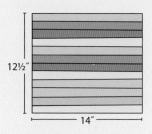

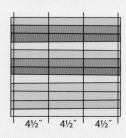

Fabric Selection

For this quilt I worked with warm colors: pinks, reds, oranges, and yellows. I wanted the quilt to be as bright and cheery as possible, so I chose fabric with clear white tones only. I refrained from using any fabric that had creamy or gray tones.

Construction

All seam allowances are ¼″ unless otherwise noted.

1. Sew the strings together side by side until the string unit is slightly larger than 4½″ × 12½″. Press the seams to one side. Use steam or spray starch to help the unit lie flat. Trim to 4½″ × 12½″. Make 72 string units.

Tip

Straighten Things Out

If your string unit looks more like an arc than a straight line, you can fix it easily. Add a wedge-shaped piece to either end (or both ends) of the unit. You may need to trim the length of the string unit before adding the end piece(s).

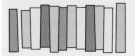

2. Arrange 2 string units and 1 background rectangle as shown. Sew the pieces together. Press. The block should measure 12½″ × 12½″ square. Make 36 blocks.

3. Using the quilt assembly diagram (next page) as a guide, arrange the blocks in a pleasing manner, rotating every other block 90°. Sew the blocks into rows. Follow the arrows for pressing directions. Sew the rows together to complete the quilt top. Press the quilt top well.

FINISHING

1. Sew around the perimeter of the quilt top ⅛″ from the edge. This will prevent the seams from splitting during handling before it is quilted.

2. Piece the back to measure at least 80″ × 80″.

3. Baste, quilt, and bind, using your preferred methods. Label if you wish.

4. Wash and dry.

Quilt assembly

June

Finished blocks: 4″ × 4″, 4″ × 8″, 8″ × 8″ • Finished quilt: 85″ × 85″

Strings are always abundant in my scrap bins, and this was a great way to use some of them up. Random placement of the scraps is ideal, so this is a good project to work on when you don't feel like thinking too much but you still want to sew. I made the quilt nice and large so my family and I can use it for picnics in the summer.

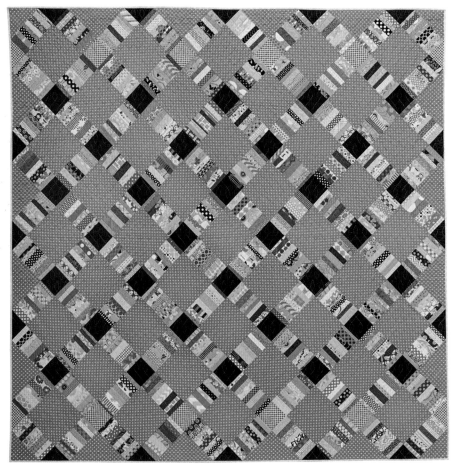

Pieced by Amanda Jean Nyberg; quilted by Steffani K. Burton

Materials

Strings approximately 1½″ × 4¾″ in a variety of colors: about 4½ yards total

Background: 2½ yards of green polka dot

Cornerstones: ¾ yard of navy solid and ⅜ yard of red gingham

Backing: 7⅞ yards

Binding: ¾ yard

Cotton batting: 93″ × 93″

Cutting

WOF = width of fabric

STRINGS

Cut (or collect) approximately 800 strings of fabric measuring about 1¼″–2″ × 4¾″.

BACKGROUND

Cut 4 squares 12⅝″ × 12⅝″.

Subcut each of the squares on the diagonal twice to make 16 quarter-square triangles. Label them A.

Cut 41 squares 8½″ × 8½″. Label them B.

Cut 2 squares 6⅝″ × 6⅝″.

Subcut each of the squares on the diagonal once to make 4 half-square triangles. Label them C.

CORNERSTONES

Navy solid

Cut 32 squares 4½″ × 4½″. Label them D.

Cut 4 squares 7″ × 7″.

Subcut each of the squares on the diagonal twice to make 16 quarter-square triangles. Label them E.

Red gingham

Cut 8 squares 4½″ × 4½″. Label them F.

Cut 1 square 7″ × 7″.

Subcut the square on the diagonal twice to make 4 quarter-square triangles. Label them G.

BINDING

Cut 9 strips 2½″ × WOF.

Fabric Selection

Almost all colors of scraps were used in this quilt. The green background was a bold choice, but I like it because it is unusual—and I selected the color during the month of June, when my entire backyard was a brilliant green. I have no doubt that that influenced my decision. For the cornerstones I used a combination of navy blue and red gingham. If I had used all navy blue, the cornerstones would have been overpowering and would have felt too heavy in relation to the rest of the quilt. Substituting some of the navy blue with the red gingham gives the quilt a more authentic, scrappy feel, and it also gives a nod to the picnic theme without going overboard.

Tip

Vary the Strip Widths

The number of strips needed for each sashing unit will vary depending on the width of each strip. The narrower the strips, the more you will need for each unit. Use wider strips on the ends to allow plenty of room for trimming.

Construction

All seam allowances are ¼″ unless otherwise noted.

1. Sew the strings together side by side until the sashing unit is slightly larger than 4½″ × 8½″. Press the seams to one side. Use steam or spray starch to help the sashing unit lie flat. Trim down to 4½″ × 8½″. Make 100 sashing units.

2. Using the quilt assembly diagram (page 86) as a guide, place the string sashing units in a pleasing arrangement on a design wall.

3. Fill in the background and cornerstone squares on the design wall.

4. Fill in the side and corner setting triangles on the design wall.

5. Sew the string sashing, squares, and triangles together into diagonal rows. Refer to Add the Triangles (next page) for the best way to attach the triangles to the sashing units. Press the seams as indicated by the arrows in the quilt assembly diagram (page 86).

6. Sew the rows together. Press the quilt top well.

About the Process

This quilt was in progress for about a year and a half—and that is okay. In fact, I had started piecing the string units before I decided on the final design. Since it spanned such a long time frame, there is a whole lot of variety in the scraps, and the quilt is better because of it.

Add the Triangles

Outside Corner Setting Triangles

1. For each of the outside corner triangles (C), fold the triangle in half and finger crease to mark the middle. Fold the sashing unit in half and finger crease to mark the middle. **Fig. A**

2. Place the pieces right sides together and align the 2 fold marks. First pin the pieces together on the fold mark. Then place pins on both ends of the triangle. Sew and press toward the triangle. **Fig. B**

3. Carefully trim the triangle tips that extend from each end of the sashing with sharp scissors or a rotary cutter. **Fig. C**

Small Setting Triangles

1. For the small setting triangles (E and G), align the pieces as shown. The triangle tip will extend a bit past the sashing. **Fig. A**

2. Place the pieces right sides together. Pin, sew, and press. **Fig. B**

3. Carefully trim the triangle tip that extends from the edge of the sashing with sharp scissors or a rotary cutter. **Fig. C**

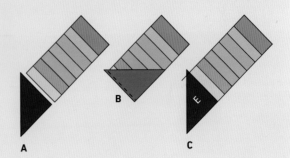

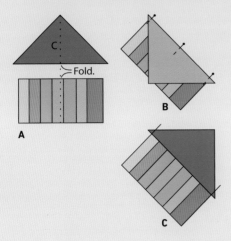

Large Setting Triangles

1. For the large setting triangles (A), align the pieces as shown. The triangle tip will extend a bit past the sashing. **Fig. A**

2. Place the pieces right sides together. Pin, sew, and press. **Fig. B**

3. Carefully trim the triangle tip that extends from the edge of the block with sharp scissors or a rotary cutter. **Fig. C**

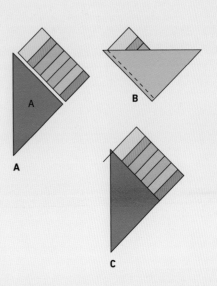

FINISHING

1. Sew around the perimeter of the quilt top ⅛″ from the edge. This will prevent the seams from splitting during handling before it is quilted.

2. Piece the back to measure at least 93″ × 93″.

3. Baste, quilt, and bind, using your preferred methods. Label if you wish.

4. Wash and dry.

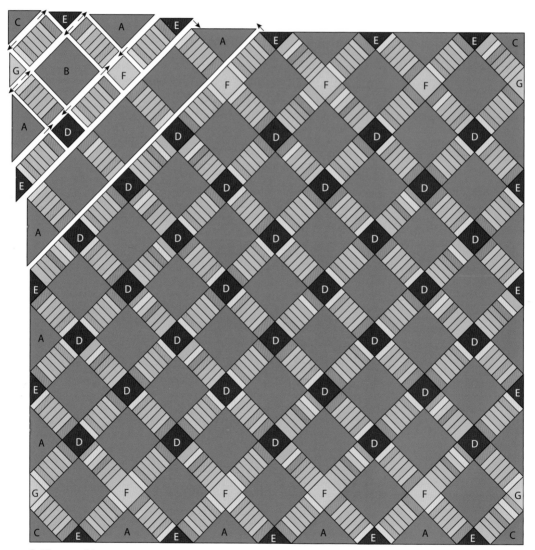

Quilt assembly

PROJECTS USING
Triangles

Chain of Diamonds

Finished block: 2″ × 2″ • Finished quilt: 50″ × 60″

This quilt uses binding triangles: the little corners that are
cut off when mitering strips of binding together. The triangles
are pieced onto the background blocks in a free-form manner.
When the blocks are assembled, the points won't necessary
align, but that is intentional. There is no need to be concerned
with precision until it's time to assemble the blocks.

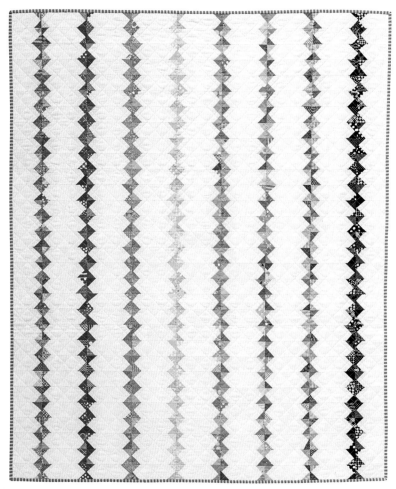

Pieced and quilted by Amanda Jean Nyberg

Materials

White and cream-colored scraps: about 3½ yards total

960 binding triangles (see project introduction, page 88), *or* **scraps of pink, red, orange, yellow, green, aqua, gray, and black:** about ⅓ yard total of each color

Backing: 3½ yards

Binding: ⅝ yard

Cotton batting: 58″ × 68″

Cutting

WOF = width of fabric

WHITE AND CREAM-COLORED SCRAPS
Cut 750 squares 2½″ × 2½″.

BINDING TRIANGLES
Collect 120 binding triangles in *each* of the following colors: pink, red, orange, yellow, green, aqua, gray, and black.

or

Cut 60 squares 2½″ × 2½″ in *each* of the following colors: pink, red, orange, yellow, green, aqua, gray, and black. Cut squares on the diagonal once, yielding 120 triangles.

Sizes May Vary

Binding widths generally vary from 2″–2½″ wide. For this quilt, I recommend using triangles cut from 2¼″- and 2½″-wide binding strips for the majority of the pieces. Triangles from binding strips that are cut 2″ wide may be used for this quilt, but I would recommend mixing them with the larger-size triangles.

BINDING
Cut 7 strips 2½″ × WOF.

Make It Faster

If you are using a single background fabric for this quilt, cut 9 strips 2½″ × 60½″ and reduce the number of background blocks to 480. Use the 2½″ strips vertically between the columns of pieced blocks.

If you would like to make this quilt but don't want to invest quite as much time as the construction directions require, consider using a larger background block. Start with a 4″ × 4″ or 5″ × 5″ square rather than a 2½″ × 2½″ square. For the colored triangles, use squares up to 1″ smaller than the background block. For example, if you are using a 5″ × 5″ background square, use a 4″ × 4″ square, cut once on the diagonal, for the triangle corners.

Fabric Selection

Various white and cream fabrics were used for the background of this quilt. If you would prefer a cleaner look, use a single fabric for the background. Use a variety of medium and dark values within each strip of color so that the diamonds sparkle. Contrast between the colored strips and the background is important so that the design has maximum impact.

Construction

All seam allowances are ¼″ unless otherwise noted.

1. Place a colored triangle on top of a white background square, right sides together. Before sewing, fold the triangle over the corner to make sure that it will cover the entire corner of the background square. Remember to account for the seam allowance. Sew ¼″ from the diagonal edge of the triangle.

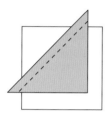

2. Fold the triangle back to cover the corner of the background fabric and press. All of the corner background fabric should be covered by the colored triangle. If some of the background fabric is still visible in the corner, the triangle will need to be repositioned and sewn again.

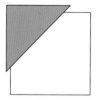

Correct triangle placement   Incorrect triangle placement

3. Trim, leaving a ¼″ seam allowance. Fold the colored triangle back to cover the trimmed corner and press well.

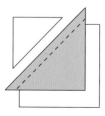

4. Place another colored triangle on the unit from Step 3, right sides together. Double-check the placement to ensure the triangle will cover the entire corner of the background fabric. Sew ¼″ from the diagonal edge of the triangle.

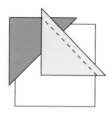

5. Check that the triangle will cover the entire corner and then trim the background fabric from behind the second colored triangle, leaving a ¼″ seam allowance. Fold the colored triangle back in place and press well. Trim the block to 2½″ × 2½″.

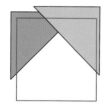

6. Repeat Steps 1–5 to make a total of 60 blocks in *each* of the colors.

7. Arrange the blocks in a pleasing manner, using the quilt assembly diagram (next page) as a guide.

8. Sew the blocks into rows. Follow the arrows for pressing directions. Sew the rows together to complete the quilt top. Press the quilt top well.

FINISHING

1. Sew around the perimeter of the quilt top ⅛″ from the edge. This will prevent the seams from splitting during handling before it is quilted.

2. Piece the back to measure at least 58″ × 68″.

3. Baste, quilt, and bind, using your preferred methods. Label if you wish.

4. Wash and dry.

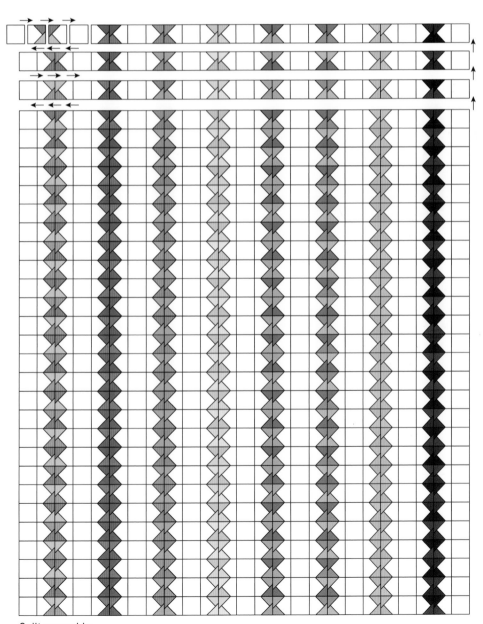

Quilt assembly

Remainders

Finished block: 2½″ × 2½″   •   Finished quilt: 60″ × 75″

A few years ago, I was sewing at a quilt retreat. A friend who
was sewing next to me asked if I wanted the trimmings from her
snowball blocks. Of course I wouldn't say no! Most of the triangles
measured about 2″ on the shortest side. They are tiny but oh so
lovely, and they were the starting point for this quilt.

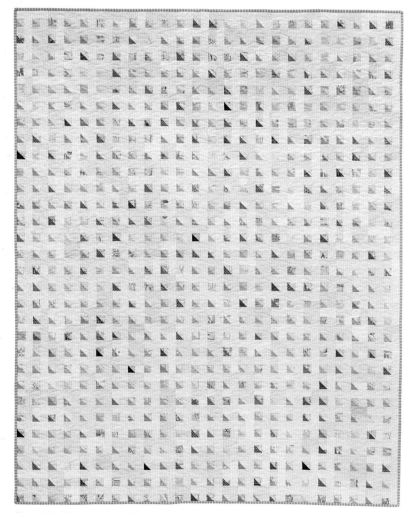

Pieced by Amanda Jean Nyberg; quilted by Steffani K. Burton

Materials

720 triangle scraps in medium/dark values: about 1¼ yards total

720 triangle scraps in light values: about 1¼ yards total

Background: cream-colored scraps, about 6½–7 yards total

Backing: 4¾ yards

Binding: ⅝ yard

Cotton batting: 68″ × 83″

Cutting

WOF = width of fabric

TRIANGLE SCRAPS

Each triangle should measure about 2″ on the shorter sides of the triangle.

Cut (or collect) 720 triangles in medium/dark values.

Cut (or collect) 720 triangles in light values.

The triangles may be a bit larger or a bit smaller than 2″; the slight variety in size adds interest to the quilt. If you don't have triangle trimmings, start by cutting 2″ × 2″ squares and then cut them on the diagonal once to make the triangles.

CREAM-COLORED BACKGROUND SCRAPS

Cut strips 2¼″ wide from various different cream-colored fabrics. Lengths may vary.

BINDING

Cut 8 strips 2½″ × WOF.

Make It Faster

If you prefer a quicker method, use larger pieces. For the triangles, try starting with a 2½″ × 2½″ square rather than a 2″× 2″ square. Increase the cut size of the border strips to 3″ wide. Trim the blocks to 4½″ × 4½″ square. Or play around with different triangle and border sizes to see what proportions you like. Make several test blocks before cutting out all the pieces of the quilt; then follow the instructions for assembling the quilt (page 98).

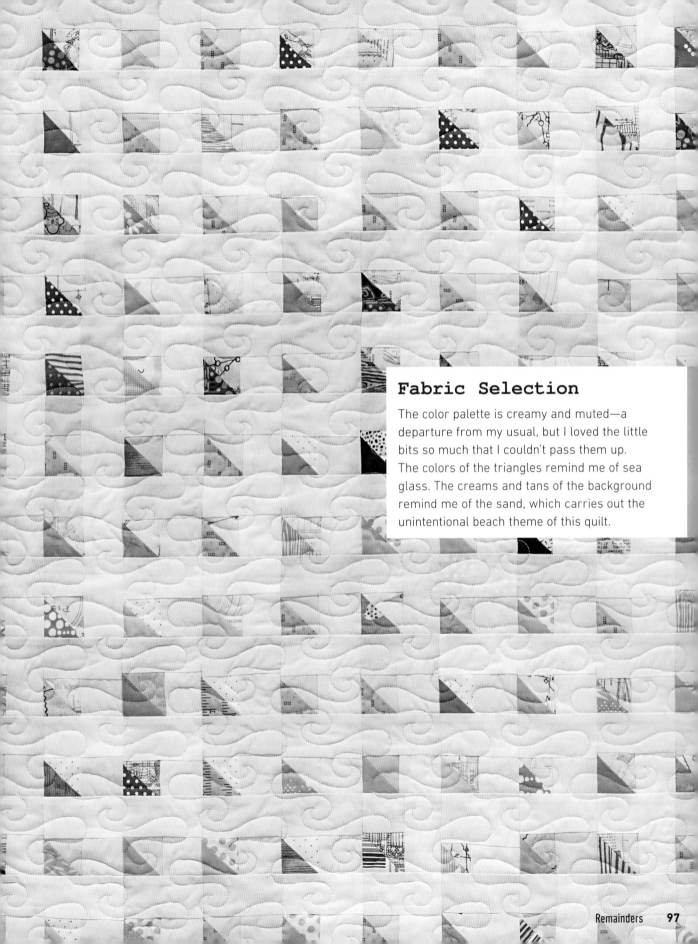

Fabric Selection

The color palette is creamy and muted—a departure from my usual, but I loved the little bits so much that I couldn't pass them up. The colors of the triangles remind me of sea glass. The creams and tans of the background remind me of the sand, which carries out the unintentional beach theme of this quilt.

Construction

All seam allowances are ¼″ unless otherwise noted.

1. Select 1 medium/dark triangle and 1 light triangle. Place them right sides together and sew along the diagonal edge. Press the seam open or to the side, whichever you prefer. Trim off the tails with sharp scissors or a rotary cutter. Repeat to make 720 half-square triangle (HST) units. The HST units will vary in size but should measure approximately 1⅝″ × 1⅝″ square.

2. Select a cream-colored strip that measures 2¼″ wide and place a half-square triangle unit, right side down, onto the strip in the exact orientation shown below. Sew it in place. Leaving a small gap, place another HST unit down on the strip and sew it in place. Repeat for as many units as will fit on the length of the strip.

Note: Pay attention to the orientation of the triangles when piecing. Always place the medium/dark triangles in the exact orientation shown in the diagrams. This will ensure that the block border strips are sewn to the correct side of the half-square triangle units.

3. Cut the bordered units apart. Press. Trim the excess border so that the strip is the same height as the half-square triangle unit. Repeat for all 720 blocks.

4. Select a cream-colored 2¼″-wide strip and place a unit from Step 3 on the strip, right side down. Once again, pay close attention to the orientation of the medium/dark triangles. Sew the unit in place. Leave a small gap, then place another unit onto the strip. Repeat for as many units as will fit on the length of the strip. Repeat for all 720 units.

5. Cut the units apart. Press the seams to the side. Trim each to 3″ × 3″ (unfinished), trimming chiefly off the cream-colored sides. Trim as little as possible from the triangle sides. Each half-square triangle block should be bordered on the right and on the top. Make 720 blocks.

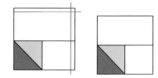

6. Arrange the blocks in a pleasing manner in a 24 by 30 block layout, using the quilt assembly diagram (page 100) as a guide.

7. Sew the blocks into rows. Follow the arrows for pressing directions. Sew the rows together to complete the quilt top. Press the quilt top well.

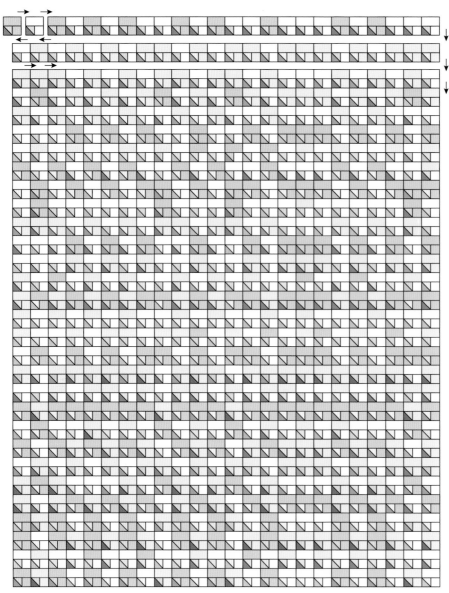

Quilt assembly

FINISHING

1. Sew around the perimeter of the quilt top ⅛″ from the edge. This will prevent the seams from splitting during handling before it is quilted.

2. Piece the back to measure at least 68″ × 83″.

3. Baste, quilt, and bind, using your preferred methods. Label if you wish.

4. Wash and dry.

PROJECTS USING
Snippets

Ring Me

Finished block: 6½" × 6½"   •   Finished quilt: 66½" × 90½"

This quilt started off with a rough idea of a Churn Dash block made with scrappy strips. I made several variations of the block, but I didn't like any of them. While I was making the pieces and parts, I discovered that I liked it best when I left the corner triangles out! I enjoyed piecing this quilt because I was able to play with so many different color combinations—and I was able to use up lots of small scraps.

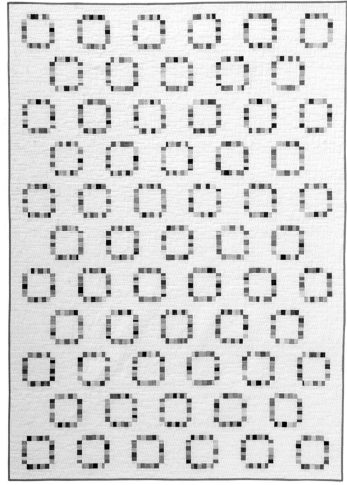

Pieced by Amanda Jean Nyberg; quilted by Steffani K. Burton

Materials

Solid scraps/snippets in a variety of colors: about 2½–3½ yards total

Background: 5½ yards

Backing: 5⅝ yards

Binding: ¾ yard

Cotton batting: 75″ × 99″

Cutting

WOF = width of fabric

SOLID SCRAPS/SNIPPETS

Cut (or collect) hundreds of pieces of fabric that measure 1″–2″ × 1½″–2″.

BACKGROUND

Cut 10 sashing strips 2″ × 68″ parallel to the selvage. Label them Y.

Cut 2 sashing strips 2½″ × 68″ parallel to the selvage. Label them Z.

Cut 50 pieces 5″ × 7″. Label them A.

Cut 10 pieces 7″ × 8½″. Label them B.

Cut 12 pieces 3″ × 7″. Label them C.

Cut 61 pieces 5″ × 5″. Label them D.

Cut 244 pieces 1½″ × 1½″. Label them E.

BINDING

Cut 9 strips 2½″ × WOF.

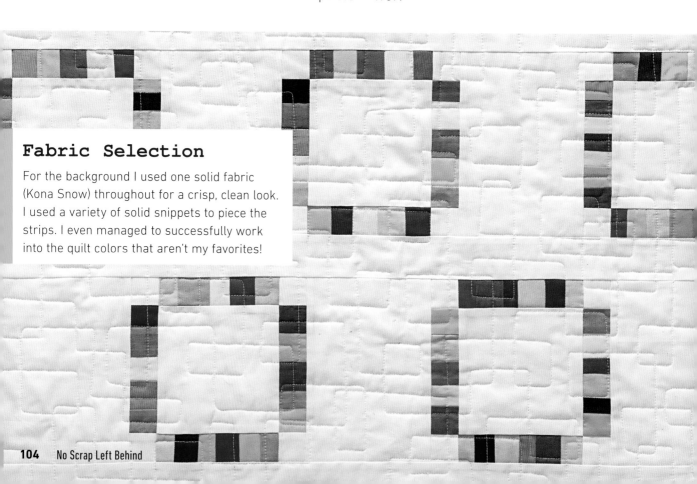

Fabric Selection

For the background I used one solid fabric (Kona Snow) throughout for a crisp, clean look. I used a variety of solid snippets to piece the strips. I even managed to successfully work into the quilt colors that aren't my favorites!

Make It Faster

Not everyone has the patience to sit and sew hundreds of tiny little pieces together. This quilt can be made more quickly by using strip-piecing methods. Sew several strips together to make a piece at least 5″ wide. The length of the strips can vary according to the scraps you have on hand. Press the seams to one side. Subcut the strip set into 1½″-wide segments. Distribute the strings that are exactly alike into several different blocks throughout the quilt.

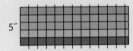

Another method is to use solid strips of fabric rather than piecing the strips. Each block can be scrappy, using various solids, or can use one color per block.

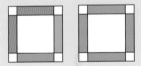

Yet another option is to use several striped fabrics in place of the pieced strings to mimic the pieced blocks without all the work.

Construction

All seam allowances are ¼″ unless otherwise noted.

1. Sew the scraps together side by side to make a string at least 1½″ × 5″. Press well. Use steam or spray starch to help the string lie flat. Press the seams open or to the side, whichever you prefer. Make 244 strings.

Tip

Use a Short Stitch Length

When making the strings, shorten the stitch length on your sewing machine to prevent the small pieces from separating during block construction.

2. Trim each string to 1½″ × 5″.

3. For each block select 4 strings, 1 D piece, and 4 E pieces. Lay them out and sew the block together in rows, as shown.

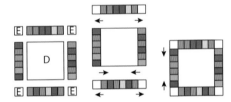

4. Repeat Step 3 to make a total of 61 blocks. Press well.

5. Place the blocks in a pleasing arrangement on a design wall. Fill in the rest of the background pieces, using the quilt assembly diagram (page 106) as a guide. Sew the blocks into rows. Follow the arrows for pressing directions.

6. Measure and record the length of each row. (If the rows are inconsistent lengths, trim all of them to the shortest length.) Trim the Y and Z pieces (originally cut to 68″ long) to match the length of your rows. Aim for 67″ long.

7. Sew the rows and sashing pieces (Y and Z) together to complete the quilt top. Press the quilt top well.

FINISHING

1. Sew around the perimeter of the quilt top ⅛″ from the edge. This will prevent the seams from splitting during handling before it is quilted.

2. Piece the quilt back to measure at least 75″ × 99″.

3. Baste, quilt, and bind, using your preferred methods. Label if you wish.

4. Wash and dry.

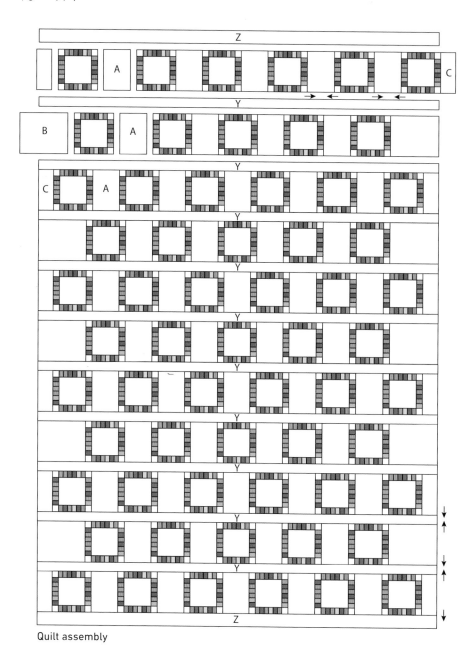

Quilt assembly

Pincushion Basics

Part of my pincushion collection

Pincushions are useful, are fun to make, and make great gifts for sewing friends. Pincushions are the perfect place to use up tiny scraps, including batting scraps. I haven't kept track of how many pincushions I've made over the years, but it's quite a few. Through trial and error, I've come up with a basic formula that produces a sturdy, soft, and smooth pincushion.

Front

For the front of my pincushions, I like to make a small patchwork block and quilt it onto a layer of batting. (No backing fabric is needed for this tiny quilt sandwich.) The batting provides a smooth sturdiness to the piece, but it still remains soft and flexible. The quilting adds texture.

Back

For the back of my pincushions I like to use quilting cotton, along with a layer of Pellon SF101 Shape-Flex interfacing. This particular interfacing is woven, with one fusible side. It is easy to work with, soft and flexible, and very helpful for adding stability to the quilting cotton.

If you prefer to skip the interfacing, another option is to use two quilted pieces to make a two-sided pincushion.

Filling

My favorite type of pincushion filling is crushed walnut shells. Sold in major pet stores as lizard litter, they add a nice weight to a pincushion, and they are supposed to sharpen your pins as you stick them into the filling. (I'm not completely sure that they help, but they certainly don't hurt.) If you have nut allergies, consider using ground emery or play sand instead of the crushed walnut shells. Pincushions up to 5″ × 5″ square are good candidates for crushed walnut-shell filling.

For large pincushions (larger than 5″ × 5″ square), I prefer to use polyfill so that the pincushion doesn't get too heavy. If you have wool roving on hand, that also makes a wonderful filling. Use a knitting needle, a chopstick, or blunt-tipped scissors to arrange the filling. Be sure to take time to fill the corners sufficiently when using polyfill or wool roving.

Hand Stitching

When it comes time to stitch the opening closed, a whipstitch is sufficient. The hand stitching virtually disappears if you use invisible thread. If you use cotton (or polyester) thread to hand stitch the opening closed, a ladder stitch is a good option for a tidy finish.

Skinny Pinnie

Finished pincushion: 2″ × 6″

This skinny little pincushion was designed to fit perfectly in the throat of my sewing machine. My pins are always close at hand, but the pincushion doesn't get in the way while I am piecing. Use these measurements as a starting point, but feel free to resize the pincushion to fit your own sewing machine.

Pieced and quilted by Amanda Jean Nyberg

Materials and Cutting

Skinny scraps in various colors: each measuring ¾″–1⅛″ × 2¾″

Interfacing: 1 piece 2½″ × 6½″ (I prefer Pellon SF101 Shape-Flex.)

Batting: 4″ × 8″

Pincushion back: 2½″ × 6½″

Crushed walnut shells or polyfill for stuffing

Invisible thread for hand stitching

Fabric Selection

The sky is the limit when it comes to fabric selection. Use whatever scraps you have on hand. Really, anything goes!

Construction

All seam allowances are ¼″ unless otherwise noted.

1. Sew the skinny scraps together side by side until the piece measures at least 2¾″ × 7″. Press the seams to one side. Trim to 2½″ × 6½″.

> ### Tip
> #### Use a Short Stitch Length
> When sewing snippets, shorten the stitch length on your sewing machine to prevent the small pieces from separating during construction.

2. Place the patchwork on top of the batting, right side up. Quilt with straight lines close to the edges of the seams. Then sew around the perimeter of the piece, very close to the outside edge, to hold the raw edges of the patchwork in place. Trim off the excess batting.

3. Fuse the interfacing to the wrong side of the back fabric according to the package directions. Use a pressing cloth to protect your iron.

4. Place the interfaced back fabric and the patchwork piece right sides together. Pin the layers together. Sew around the perimeter, leaving a 2″–3″ gap open for turning. Backstitch at the beginning and end of the seam.

5. Trim the corners close to the seamline, taking care not to trim through it. Turn the piece right side out. Press.

6. Fill the pincushion with crushed walnut shells or polyfill.

7. Using invisible thread, hand stitch the opening closed with a whipstitch.

Make It Larger

Finished pincushion: 2½″ × 8½″

This skinny pinnie is the perfect size for placing right in front of your sewing machine. For this larger version, piece the patchwork panel to about 3¼″ × 9¼″. Press the seams to one side. Trim the piece down to 3″ × 9″ (see Step 1, above). Cut the backing and interfacing pieces 3″ × 9″. Quilt and assemble as directed above.

Needle Sorter

Finished needle sorter: 3″ × 6½″

After sewing through paper, whether for a paper-piecing
project or if you are making cards (page 124), your sewing
machine needle will become dull. It's a great idea to keep
the needles used for sewing through fabric and sewing
through paper separate. Needles that are too dull to sew
through fabric still work well for sewing through paper. Use
this cute cushion to keep them separated and organized.

Quilted and pieced by Amanda Jean Nyberg

Materials and Cutting

Small scraps/snippets in various colors: each measuring ¾"–1¼" × 1¼"

White: 2 squares 3½" × 3½"

Interfacing: 2 squares 3½" × 3½" and 1 piece 3½" × 7" (I prefer Pellon SF101 Shape-Flex.)

Batting: 4" × 8"

Pincushion back: 1 piece 3½" × 7"

Crushed walnut shells *or* **polyfill for stuffing**

Invisible thread for hand stitching

Light blue thread

Red quilting thread for the lettering *or* **embroidery floss for hand stitching**

Optional: Transfer product, such as Wash-Away Stitch Stabilizer (by C&T Publishing)

Construction

All seam allowances are ¼" unless otherwise noted.

1. Fuse the 3½" × 3½" squares of interfacing to the wrong side of the white squares according to the package directions. Use a pressing cloth to protect your iron.

2. Use the light blue thread to quilt straight lines on the white squares. Space the lines approximately ¼" apart to mimic notebook paper.

3. Use red quilting thread and a free-motion foot to "write" the words *fabric* and *paper* onto the center of the white squares. Use the "notebook lines" as a guide for the lettering. If you are not comfortable with free-motion quilting, copy or trace the words (page 115) onto the Wash-Away Stitch Stabilizer and use embroidery floss to hand stitch the words instead.

Tip

Practice Makes Better

Getting the lettering just right can be little bit tricky. Practice quilting the words on scrap fabric several times before attempting to make the final blocks. Try a variety of thread weights to see what works best in your machine. Make a sample of both the machine stitching and the hand stitching to see which one yields the best results for you.

Fabric Selection

Use bright-colored scraps for the patchwork borders and white or cream-colored fabric for the center blocks.

4. Trim the white blocks down to 3″ wide × 2½″ tall, centering the words *fabric* and *paper* as much as possible.

5. Sew small scraps together side by side until the piece measures at least 1¼″ × 2¾″. Press the seams to one side. Trim the piece to 1″ × 2½″. Repeat this step to make 3 total.

Tip

Use a Short Stitch Length

When sewing snippets, shorten the stitch length on your sewing machine to prevent the small pieces from separating during construction.

6. Sew small scraps together side by side until the piece measures at least 1¼″ × 7½″. Press the seams to one side. Trim the piece to 1″ × 7″. Repeat this step to make 2 total.

7. Arrange the pieces as shown.

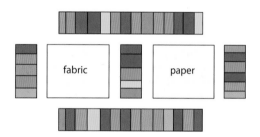

8. Sew the short patchwork strips to the embroidered squares to make a row. Press the seams to one side. Sew the 1″ × 7″ strips to the top and bottom of the piece. Press the seams to one side.

9. Place the patchwork on the piece of batting right side up. Quilt with straight lines close to the edges of the patchwork strips. Then sew around the perimeter of the piece, very close to the outside edge, to hold the raw edges of the patchwork in place. Trim off the excess batting.

10. Fuse the interfacing to the wrong side of the cushion back according to the package directions. Use a pressing cloth to protect your iron.

11. Place the interfaced back and the patchwork piece right sides together. Pin the layers together. Sew around the perimeter, leaving a 2″–3″ gap open for turning. Backstitch at the beginning and end of the seam.

12. Trim the corners close to the seamline, taking care not to trim through it. Turn right side out. Press.

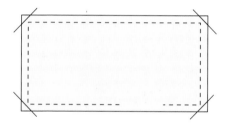

13. Fill the needle sorter with crushed walnut shells or polyfill.

14. Using invisible thread, hand stitch the opening closed with a whipstitch.

fabric

paper

fabric

paper

Bright Birch Tree Pincushion

Finished pincushion: 4″ × 4″

This little pincushion was inspired by a quilt that I made several years ago. The pieces are small, but that's what makes it so charming. Don't let the small pieces scare you—the project still comes together quickly. Make several pincushions, one to keep and the rest to share with your sewing friends!

Pieced and quilted by Amanda Jean Nyberg

Fabric Selection

Choose a variety of bright colors for the pieced tree trunks and pair with a background of Essex linen (from Robert Kaufman Fabrics). Or piece a variety of light-colored scraps for the tree trunks and pair with a bold solid-colored background. Mix and match color combinations to your liking.

Materials and Cutting

Tiny scraps in various colors: each measuring ¾″–1⅛″ × 1⅛″

Background: 1 square 5″ × 5″

Batting: 1 square 5″ × 5″

Pincushion back: 1 square 4½″ × 4½″

Interfacing: 1 square 4½″ × 4½″ (I prefer Pellon SF101 Shape-Flex.)

Crushed walnut shells or polyfill for stuffing

Invisible thread for hand stitching

Construction

All seam allowances are ¼″ unless otherwise noted.

1. Sew small scraps together side by side until the piece measures at least 1⅛″ × 5½″ long. Press the seams to one side. Repeat this step to make 3 strips total.

Tip

Use a Short Stitch Length

When sewing snippets, shorten the stitch length on your sewing machine to prevent the small pieces from separating during construction.

2. Trim the strips to 1″ wide. Plan the arrangement of the strips on the background square.

3. Make the first cut in the background square, starting the cut 1″ from the top left-hand corner and angling slightly to the right.

4. Sew the 3 pieces together to insert the first strip into the background. Press the seams toward the background.

5. Make the second cut in the background square, angling the cut slightly in the middle of the background fabric.

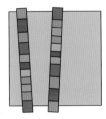

6. Sew the 3 pieces together to insert the second strip into the background. Press the seams toward the background fabric.

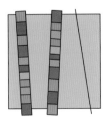

7. Make the third cut in the background square, angling the cut slightly and ending about 1″ from the lower right-hand corner.

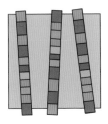

8. Sew the 3 pieces together to insert the third strip into the background. Press the seams toward the background fabric. Trim the patchwork to 4½″ × 4½″ square.

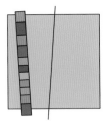

9. Center the birch tree block on the 5″ × 5″ square of batting, right side up. Quilt with straight lines close to the edges of the patchwork strips. Then sew around the perimeter of the piece, very close to the outside edge, to hold the raw edges of the patchwork in place. Trim off the excess batting.

10. Fuse the interfacing to the wrong side of the back fabric according to the package directions. Use a pressing cloth to protect your iron.

11. Place the interfaced back fabric and the birch tree block right sides together. Pin the layers together. Sew around the perimeter, leaving a 2″–3″ gap open for turning. Backstitch at the beginning and end of the seam.

12. Trim the corners close to the seamline, taking care not to trim through it. Turn right side out. Press.

13. Fill the pincushion with crushed walnut shells or polyfill.

14. Using invisible thread, hand stitch the opening closed with a whipstitch.

Pillow Pincushion

Finished pincushion: 8″ × 8½″

This oversized pincushion is quite handy. The large size makes
it hard to miss when it's time to use it—you don't need to
really aim, just point your pins in the general direction of the
pincushion. The size of the pincushion also makes it hard to
lose under piles of fabric.

Pieced and quilted by Amanda Jean Nyberg

Fabric Selection

Choose a variety of fabrics for
the patchwork. Perhaps highlight
scraps from your favorite fabric
designer, or celebrate a certain
type of print, such as polka dots,
as I did here. Try using plaids,
stripes, or even a variety of solids.

Materials and Cutting

Small scraps in a variety of colors:
each measuring 1¼″–2″ × 2½″

Batting: 1 square 10″ × 10″

Pincushion back: 1 piece 8½″ × 9″

Interfacing: 1 piece 8½″ × 9″
(I prefer Pellon SF101 Shape-Flex.)

1 small button for the bottom of the pincushion

1 large button for the top of the pincushion

Embroidery floss or perle cotton

Extra-large sewing needle

Polyfill for stuffing

Invisible thread for hand stitching

Construction

All seam allowances are ¼″ unless otherwise noted.

1. Sew scraps together side by side until the strip measures 2½″ × 9½″. Press the seams to one side. Trim the strip to 2¼″-wide. Repeat this step to make 5 strips total.

> ### Tip
>
> ### Use a Short Stitch Length
> When sewing snippets, shorten the stitch length on your sewing machine to prevent the small pieces from separating during construction.

2. Arrange the 5 patchwork strips as desired. Sew the strips together. Press the seams to one side. Trim the piece to 8½″ × 9″.

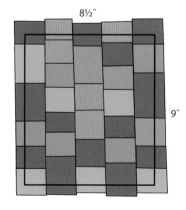

8½″

9″

3. Center the piece of patchwork on the square of batting, right side up. Quilt with straight lines close to the edges of the patchwork strips. Then sew around the perimeter of the piece, very close to the outside edge, to hold the raw edges of the patchwork in place. Trim off the excess batting.

4. Fuse the interfacing to the wrong side of the back fabric according to the package directions. Use a pressing cloth to protect your iron.

5. Place the interfaced back fabric and the patchwork piece right sides together. Pin the layers together. Sew around the perimeter, leaving a 2″–3″ gap open for turning. Backstitch at the beginning and end of the seam.

6. Trim the corners close to the seamline, taking care not to trim through it. Turn right side out. Press.

7. Fill the pincushion with polyfill.

8. Using invisible thread, hand stitch the opening closed with a whipstitch.

9. Use the extra-large sewing needle and the embroidery floss or perle cotton to sew through the middle of the pincushion. Pull the thread tight to compress the middle. Attach a button on each side of the pincushion. Hide the knot and thread ends under the bottom button.

Cards

Finished card: 5½″ × 4¼″

Sewing through paper is so much fun. Use tiny fabric scraps to make a card that will bring a smile to someone's face. This is a great way to use scraps that are so small that they can no longer hold a seam allowance. This is just one example of a design. Get creative and come up with your own designs, too.

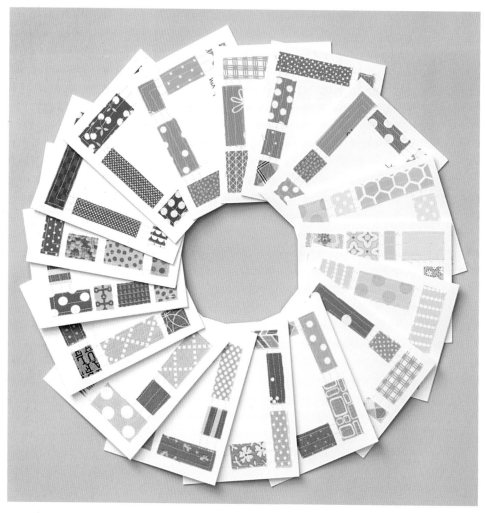

Made by Amanda Jean Nyberg

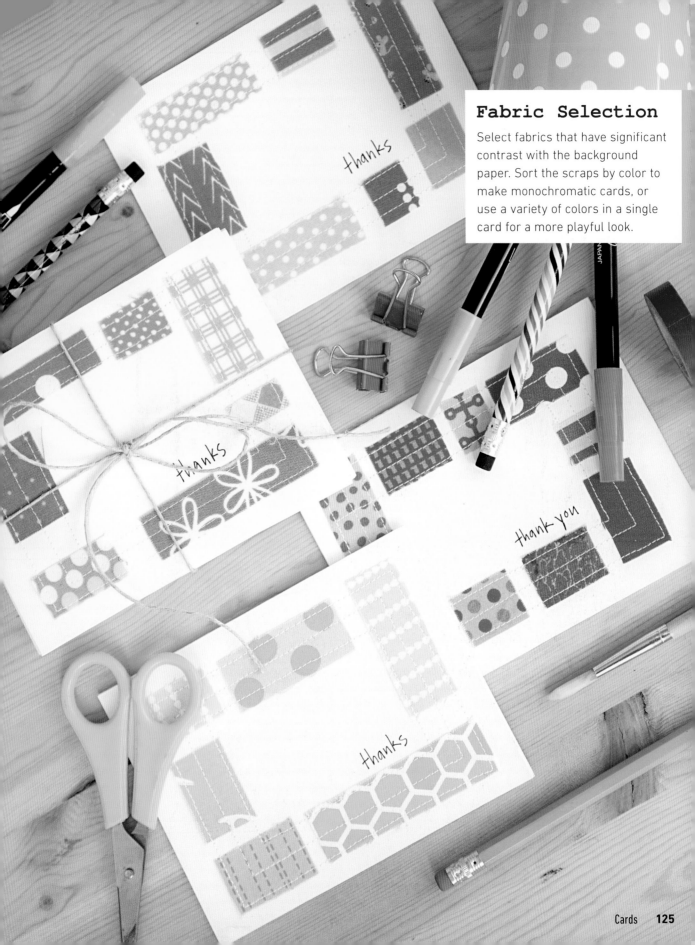

Fabric Selection

Select fabrics that have significant contrast with the background paper. Sort the scraps by color to make monochromatic cards, or use a variety of colors in a single card for a more playful look.

thanks

thanks

thank you

thanks

Materials

Small scraps in a variety of colors: each measuring ½″–1½″ on each side

8½″ × 11″ card stock

Thread to match the card stock

Glue stick

Double-sided tape or a tape runner (normally used for scrapbooking)

Construction

1. Cut a piece of card stock to 5½″ × 8½″. Fold it in half so that it measures 5½″ × 4¼″. Set aside.

2. Cut a piece of card stock to 5½″ × 4¼″.

> ### Tip
>
> ### Cutting Paper with a Rotary Cutter
>
> Use rotary cutter blades that have become too dull to cut fabric to cut paper instead. This is a great way to cut the card stock pieces quickly and accurately. Consider keeping an extra rotary cutter on hand especially for paper. And be sure to label it.

3. Arrange the scraps of fabric on the 5½″ × 4¼″ piece of card stock. Use a glue stick to hold the fabric pieces in place temporarily.

4. Stitch around the fabric edges to attach the fabric pieces to the card stock permanently. Backstitch (2 or 3 stitches is plenty) at the beginning and end of each seam. Trim the threads as short as possible.

5. Attach the patchwork piece of card stock to the folded card stock with double-sided tape or a tape runner. This will hide the stitching lines and produce a nicely finished card.

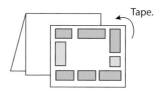

Tape.

6. Write a greeting on the front of the card (such as "hello," "thank you," or "happy birthday"), if desired.

7. Write a message inside and send the card to a friend.

> ### Tip
>
> ### Change Your Needle
>
> When you are finished making cards, be sure to change out your sewing needle, which will have become dull after sewing through paper. Store the needle in a needle sorter (page 111) until your next paper sewing project.

About the Author

Photo by Laurie Middendorf

AMANDA JEAN NYBERG, scrap quilter to the core, began her quilting journey in the year 2000. Since that first quilt for her son, she's finished nearly 300 quilts!

Amanda is a quilt teacher, fabric and pattern designer, Craftsy instructor, blogger, and coauthor of *Sunday Morning Quilts* (by C&T Publishing). She is constantly looking for new and innovative ways to turn scraps into beautiful finished objects. She tries to waste nothing.

When she isn't quilting, Amanda enjoys knitting, fishing, and spending time with her family. She also enjoys cooking and is on a quest to make *the* perfect pot of soup. Amanda lives in Minnesota with her patient husband and three rapidly growing children.

crazymomquilts.net

Also by Amanda Jean Nyberg:

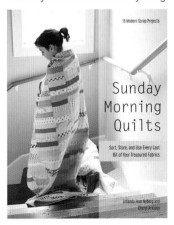

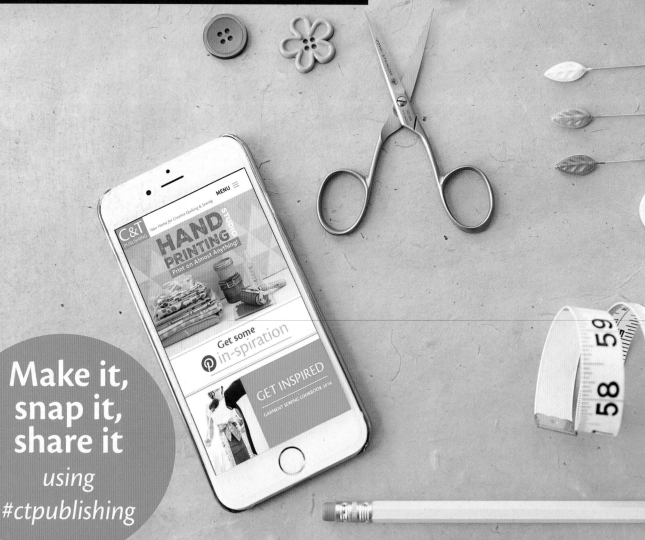

Want even more creative content?

Make it, snap it, share it
using #ctpublishing